HOT & SPICY COOKING

D1328615

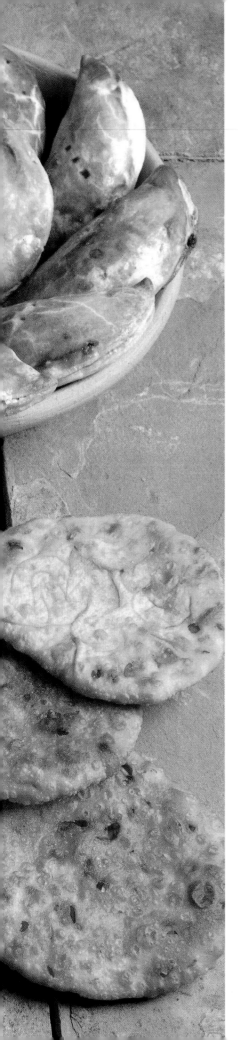

SOUPS AND SAVOURIES

Traditional Indian fare, these are also served as main courses. You'll find them delightful as appetisers or entrees.

Peanut Kachuri

PASTRY

3 cups plain flour

¼ tspn baking powder

¼ tspn salt

1 tblspn butter or margarine, softened

cold water to mix

FILLING

2 tblspns oil

1 onion, finely chopped

½ tspn chilli powder

1 cup peanuts, chopped

1 tspn chopped fresh coriander

2 tspns lemon juice

¼ tspn brown sugar

1 tblspn natural yoghurt

1 tblspn mango or other fruit chutney

salt to taste

extra flour

oil for deep frying

1 Sift flour, baking powder and salt into a mixing bowl. Add butter or margarine and using your fingertips rub into the flour until mixture resembles fine breadcrumbs. Gradually add enough cold water to mix to a firm dough, knead lightly, cover with plastic wrap and set aside for about two hours.

2 Heat oil in a heavy-based frying pan, add onion and chilli powder and cook for 3 minutes or until onion has softened slightly. Stir in peanuts, coriander, lemon juice and brown sugar, cook for 1 minute. Remove pan from heat and stir in yoghurt, chutney and salt.

3 Pinch off pieces of pastry and roll into small balls.

4 Roll out on a lightly floured board to about 10 cm (4 in) in diameter and 3 mm (⅛ in) thickness.

5 Place heaped teaspoonsful of filling onto centre of each pastry round, draw up edges and pinch together firmly to seal.

6 Dust with flour and roll out again gently to about 1 cm thickness.

7 Heat oil in a large, heavy-based saucepan or deep fryer and fry Kachuri 3 or 4 at a time until golden brown, about 4 minutes. Drain on absorbent paper and serve hot.

Makes about 24

Clockwise from top left: Pappadams (page 69), Curried Meat Crescents (page 4), Peanut Kachuri and Guli Kebabs (page 4).

Curried Meat Crescents

1 tblspn oil

1 small onion, finely chopped

1 green apple, peeled, cored and chopped

1 medium carrot, peeled and finely chopped

2 tspns curry powder

¼ tspn cinnamon

250g (8oz) topside mince or ground beef

3 tspns soy sauce

2 tblspns sultanas

3 tblspns unsalted peanuts

salt and pepper

8 sheets ready-rolled shortcrust pastry

1 egg, lightly beaten

1 Heat oil in a heavy-based saucepan; add onion, apple, carrot, curry powder and cinnamon, and fry over moderate heat for 10 minutes, or until vegetables are soft, stirring occasionally.

2 Add meat to pan and fry, pressing down with a fork for a further 5 to 7 minutes or until meat is cooked and liquid has evaporated.

3 Stir in soy sauce, sultanas and peanuts, and season to taste with salt and pepper. Cool.

4 Using a scone cutter or a glass, cut pastry into 8cm (3in) rounds. Place a teaspoonful of meat mixture on to the centre of each pastry round.

5 Brush edge of pastry with beaten egg and fold pastry over to form a semi-circle; press edges firmly together. Prick each pastry all over with a fork.

6 Place the pastries on a lightly greased baking tray and brush with the beaten egg. Bake in a hot oven (200ºC) for 15 minutes or until golden brown.

Makes about 70 crescents

Guli Kebab

500g (1lb) minced or ground steak

1 tblspn natural yoghurt

1 clove garlic, crushed

1 onion, grated

1 tspn chilli powder

1 tspn ground ginger

1 tspn garam masala

2 tspns brown sugar

½ tspn salt

2 slices bread, crusts removed

water

1 tblspn flour

½ tspn cumin

2 eggs, lightly beaten

dried breadcrumbs for coating

oil for frying

1 Place mince, yoghurt, garlic, onion, chilli powder, ginger, garam masala, brown sugar and salt in a large bowl and mix until ingredients are well combined. Cover and set aside for 2 hours.

2 Soak bread in water to cover for 1 minute. Squeeze bread to remove excess liquid and add to mince mixture with flour and cumin, mix well.

3 Roll mixture into small oval shapes.

4 Dip in beaten egg, then coat with breadcrumbs, pressing crumbs on firmly. Chill for 30 minutes.

5 Heat oil in a deep, heavy-based saucepan or deep fryer and fry meat rolls until golden brown, about 5 minutes.

6 Drain on absorbent paper and serve hot with your favourite chutney or chilli sauce.

Makes about 36 kebabs

Tangy Apple Soup

4 large green apples, peeled, cored and sliced

2¾ cups apple juice

2 chicken stock cubes

grated rind and juice of 1 lemon

¼ tspn cinnamon

1 tspn grated fresh root ginger

1 tspn curry powder

3 tspns sugar

1 tblspn dry sherry

salt and pepper

1 Place sliced apples, apple juice, chicken stock cubes, lemon rind and juice, cinnamon, ginger and curry powder in a large saucepan.

2 Bring to the boil, then lower the heat and simmer without a lid for 10 minutes or until apples are soft. Stir in the sugar.

3 Pour apple mixture into an electric blender or food processor and process until smooth, or push the apples through a sieve.

4 Pour pureed mixture into a large bowl. Stir in the sherry and season to taste with salt and pepper. Chill for several hours before serving.

Serves 4

Chilli Lentil Soup

1 tblspn oil

1 onion, finely chopped

1 tspn turmeric

2 fresh chillies, seeded and diced

4 cups chicken stock

1 cup red lentils, rinsed

salt and pepper to taste

1 Heat oil in a large, heavy-based saucepan. Add onion, turmeric and chillies and fry over low heat for 5 minutes or until onion has softened slightly.

2 Add stock and lentils, bring to the boil.

3 Lower heat, cover pan with a lid and simmer for 45 minutes to 1 hour or until lentils are tender. Season to taste with salt and pepper if necessary.

Serves 6

Clockwise from top left: Chilli Lentil Soup, Spicy Chicken Soup (page 6) and Tangy Apple Soup.

Spicy Chicken Soup

2 tblspns butter, margarine or ghee

½ cup sliced spring onions or scallions

1 green apple, peeled, cored and diced

2 carrots, peeled and diced

2 tspns curry powder

2 tblspns plain flour

6 cups chicken stock

1 cup cooked shredded chicken

1 tblspn snipped chives

⅓ cup cream

salt and pepper

1 Melt butter or margarine in a large saucepan. Add the spring onions (scallions), apple and carrots and cook over low heat, covered with a lid, until vegetables have softened and are golden brown, about 10 minutes.

2 Stir in the curry powder and flour and cook stirring for a further 2 minutes, being careful not to let the mixture burn.

3 Add the chicken stock and simmer gently without a lid for 20 minutes. Cool slightly.

4 Pour soup into an electric blender or food processor and process until pureed. Return to saucepan.

5 Stir in the chicken, chives and cream and heat through. Season to taste with salt and pepper.

6 Serve sprinkled with snipped chives.

Serves 4–6

Samosas

2 tblspns oil or ghee

1 onion, finely chopped

1 clove garlic, crushed

¼ tspn ground coriander

¼ tspn ground cumin

¼ tspn chilli powder

½ tspn turmeric

125 g (4 oz) potatoes, peeled and diced

60 g (2 oz) carrots, peeled and diced

125 g (4 oz) frozen peas, thawed

1 tspn salt

½ tspn brown sugar

1 tblspn chicken stock or water

1 pkt ready-rolled frozen puff pasty, thawed

oil for deep frying

1 Heat oil or ghee in a heavy-based saucepan, add the onion and garlic and fry until onion softens, about 5 minutes. Add the spices and cook, stirring constantly, for 2 minutes.

2 Drop the diced potatoes and carrots into a small pan of boiling salted water and boil for 2 minutes. Drain well.

3 Add all the vegetables, salt, sugar and chicken stock to the spice and onion mixture. Mix until well combined.

4 Cover the pan with a lid, return to the heat and simmer gently until all vegetables are tender, about 5 minutes. Remove the pan from the heat and allow the mixture to cool.

5 Lightly flour a board or work surface and place the sheets of pastry onto the surface. Using a lightly floured 10 cm (4 in) cutter, cut the pastry into rounds.

6 Place a teaspoonful of the vegetable mixture onto each round of pastry. Dampen the edges of the rounds lightly with water. Fold the pastry over the filling to form a semi-circle. Seal edges with the tines of a fork. Chill for 30 minutes.

7 Heat oil in a deep fryer or deep, heavy-based saucepan. When hot add the samosas a few at a time and fry until golden brown on both sides, about 2–3 minutes. When cooked, drain on absorbent paper and serve hot.

Makes about 25

Spicy Chicken Soup

Curried Eggs

45 g (1½ oz) butter or margarine

1 small onion, finely chopped

1 cooking apple, finely chopped

1 tspn curry powder

2 tblspns plain flour

2½ cups chicken stock

1 tblspn fruit chutney

1 tblspn brown sugar

juice of ½ lemon

½ tspn salt

2 tblspns sultanas

8 hard-boiled eggs

1 Melt butter or margarine in a heavy-based saucepan.

2 Add onion and apple and cook until onion has softened slightly, about 5 minutes.

3 Stir in curry powder and flour, cook for 2 minutes then gradually add stock and bring to the boil.

4 Add remaining ingredients except eggs, cover and simmer for 10 minutes.

5 Shell eggs, cut in halves and arrange on a hot serving dish.

6 Pour over sauce and serve with boiled rice and chutney.

Serves 4–6

Spicy Potato Nut Bites

FILLING

3 tblspns fresh white breadcrumbs

½ cup chopped peanuts

½ cup natural yoghurt

500 g (1 lb) potatoes, cooked, peeled and mashed

3 tblspns milk

3 tblspns finely chopped spring onions or scallions

1 egg yolk

1 tspn curry powder

salt and pepper to taste

TO COOK

flour for coating

1 egg, lightly beaten

2 cups dry breadcrumbs

oil for deep drying

1 Place breadcrumbs, peanuts and yoghurt in a small bowl and mix until well combined. Set aside.

2 Place the mashed potatoes, milk, spring onions (scallions), egg yolk and curry powder in a large mixing bowl. Mix until combined, then season with salt and pepper.

3 Take heaped tablespoonful of potato mixture and mould into croquette shapes about 8 cm (3 in) long and 3 cm (1½ in) wide, then flatten croquette slightly in your palm. Place a teaspoonful of the peanut mixture in the centre. Mould the potato around the peanut filling and reshape into a croquette.

4 Coat lightly with flour, shaking off any excess. Dip croquettes in beaten egg, then coat well with the breadcrumbs, pressing them on firmly. Chill prepared croquettes for 30 minutes, or until firm.

5 Heat oil in a deep fryer or deep, heavy-based saucepan. When oil is hot, lower croquettes a few at a time into oil using a slotted spoon. Fry until golden brown all over, about 3 minutes. Drain on absorbent paper and serve.

Makes about 12

Curried Chicken Triangles

2 rashers bacon, rinds removed and bacon chopped

2 onions, chopped

1 large potato, peeled and chopped

1 tomato, peeled and chopped

1 tspn curry powder

½ tspn cinnamon

½ cup chicken stock

2 cups cooked, chopped chicken

1 tblspn chopped parsley

1 tblspn chopped fresh mint

salt and pepper to taste

4 sheets ready-rolled puff pastry

1 egg, beaten

sesame seeds for sprinkling

1 Fry the bacon in a dry, heavy-based saucepan until the fat starts to run.

2 Add the onion, potato and tomato and fry until the vegetables soften, about 5 minutes.

3 Add the curry powder and cinnamon and fry for a further 1–2 minutes.

4 Add the stock and chicken. Mix well, bring to the boil, then lower heat and simmer for 1–2 minutes.

5 Add the parsley, mint, salt and pepper to taste. Allow to cool slightly.

6 Cut each sheet of pastry into 4 triangles. Place a tablespoonful of the mixture in the centre of each triangle. Fold pastry over to form smaller triangles. Seal edges with a fork.

7 Place the filled triangles on dampened baking trays. Brush with beaten egg and sprinkle with sesame seeds. Bake in a hot oven (200ºC) for about 20 minutes.

Makes 16 triangles

Mulligatawny Soup

size 15 (3 lb) boiling chicken

3 litres (6 pints) water

1 bouquet garni

1 tblspn butter or margarine

2 onions, thinly sliced

1 cup diced carrot

1 cup chopped celery

2 tspns curry powder

1 cup rice

salt and pepper

1 Wash chicken and remove giblets. Place chicken in a large, deep saucepan, add water and bouquet garni and cover pan with a lid. Bring to the boil, lower heat and simmer for 1½ hours, or until chicken is tender.

2 Remove chicken from pan and allow to cool, then cut flesh into small pieces.

3 Skim any excess fat from stock or, if possible, refrigerate overnight, then remove solidified fat with a knife. Reserve the chicken stock.

4 Heat butter or margarine in a large heavy-based pan, add onions, carrots, celery and curry powder and fry over low heat for 5 minutes, or until vegetables are beginning to soften.

5 Add rice and 12 cups of reserved chicken stock and bring to the boil. Lower heat and simmer for a further 20 minutes, or until rice is cooked and vegetables are tender.

6 Add chicken and season to taste with salt and pepper. Continue simmering a further 5 minutes or until chicken is heated through.

Note: Bouquet garni can be purchased in sachets from your local supermarket or delicatessen.

Serves 6

Pork and Chick Pea Soup

1 cup dried chick peas

3 tblspns oil

2 large onions, chopped

1 clove garlic, crushed

½–1 tspn chilli powder

500 g (1 lb) pork shoulder, cubed

3 tblspns plain flour

1 stalk celery, chopped

6 cups chicken stock

salt and pepper

2 tblspns chopped parsley

1 tspn chopped fresh chilli

1 Place chick peas in a large bowl, cover with water and soak overnight.

2 Drain well. Heat oil in a large, heavy-based saucepan, add onion, garlic and chilli powder and fry over moderate heat until onion has softened slightly, about 2 minutes.

3 Toss pork pieces in flour and add to pan, fry for a further 5 minutes or until pork changes colour.

4 Add drained chick peas, celery and chicken stock and bring to the boil. Lower heat, cover pan with a lid and simmer for 1–1¼ hours or until pork and chick peas are cooked.

5 Skim off any fat or oil from soup during cooking. Season to taste with salt and pepper and sprinkle with parsley and fresh chilli if liked.

Note: As soup may thicken on standing overnight, a little extra water may need to be added. If made the day before, refrigerate and lift the fat from the top of the soup with a knife.

Serves 6

Curried Pumpkin Soup

80 g (2½ oz) butter or margarine

3 tspns curry powder

2 onions, roughly chopped

4 cups chicken stock

1 kg (2 lb) peeled pumpkin, cut into pieces

salt and pepper

¼ cup sour cream

1 Melt butter or margarine in a large, heavy-based saucepan, add curry powder and onions. Fry, stirring occasionally, for 4 minutes, or until onion has softened slightly.

2 Add stock and pumpkin, and bring to the boil. Lower heat, cover pan with a lid and simmer until pumpkin is tender, about 35 minutes.

3 Remove pan from heat and cool soup slightly. Pour into an electric blender or food processor and process until pureed. You will have to do this in a few batches.

4 Season to taste with salt and pepper and swirl in the sour cream. Reheat soup gently, do not boil.

Serves 6

FISH AND SHELLFISH

The scope extends way beyond the familiar prawn curry. Some of the most delicate dishes from Asia and the Pacific use fish as a base.

Scallops in Chilli Sauce

500 g (1 lb) scallops

2 tblspns oil

2 tspns finely chopped fresh root ginger

1 clove garlic, crushed

4 spring onions or scallions, sliced diagonally

1 small red chilli, seeded and finely chopped

1 red capsicum (red pepper), seeded and cut into chunks

1 tblspn soy sauce

¼ cup chicken stock

1 tspn cornflour

1 Wash scallops, removing any dirt and pat dry with absorbent paper.

2 Heat half the oil in a wok, add scallops and cook stirring for 2 minutes or until scallops are just beginning to turn white. Remove from pan, drain off excess liquid and keep warm.

3 Add remaining oil to the wok, add ginger, garlic, onions, chilli and capsicum and cook for 1 minute or until vegetables have softened slightly but not browned.

4 Add soy sauce and stock. Bring to the boil.

5 Mix cornflour to a smooth paste with a little water and add to the wok. Cook stirring until sauce boils and thickens, about 3 minutes.

6 Add the scallops and cook for a further 2 minutes or until scallops are heated through. Serve hot.

Serves 4

Crab Lettuce Rolls

2 tspns oil

2 cloves garlic, crushed

1 onion, finely chopped

¼ tspn ground chilli pepper

⅓ cup crunchy peanut butter

1 tblspn soy sauce

1 tblspn brown sugar

½ cup water

170 g (6 oz) can crab meat, drained

4 spring onions or scallions, sliced diagonally

12 lettuce leaves, washed

1 Heat oil in a large, heavy-based frying pan or saucepan. Add garlic, onion and chilli powder and fry over moderate heat until onion has softened slightly, about 3 minutes.

Scallops in Chilli Sauce

10

2 Add all remaining ingredients (except lettuce) and cook over low heat until ingredients are well combined and sauce is thick. Remove from heat and set aside.

3 Place lettuce leaves in a large saucepan of boiling water and cook for 10–15 seconds or until wilted. Drain on absorbent paper.

4 Place each lettuce leaf flat on a board or work surface. Trim core from each leaf. Place 1–2 heaped tablespoonful of the filling on one end of each lettuce leaf.

5 Fold core end of lettuce over filling, tuck in the sides then roll up firmly to form a neat sausage-shaped roll, about 10 cm (4 in) long. Repeat with remaining lettuce leaves and filling.

Makes 12

Seafood and Fruit Kebabs

250 g (½ lb) firm white fish fillets

250 g (½ lb) scallops or peeled green prawns (or a combination)

2 onions

MARINADE

½ cup coconut cream

1 tblspn soy sauce

1 tspn grated fresh root ginger

1 clove garlic, crushed

½ tspn ground coriander

1 tspn curry powder

TO ASSEMBLE

4 bacon rashers

1 small pawpaw or 1 large rockmelon

1 Cut fish into large chunky pieces. Place in a bowl with the scallops or prawns.

2 Peel onions, cut into quarters and separate into wedges. Place onion wedges in a saucepan and cover with water. Bring to the boil, simmer for 2 minutes then drain and add to the seafood.

3 Mix coconut cream with remaining marinade ingredients and pour over the seafood and onions. Cover the bowl with plastic wrap and chill for 1–2 hours.

4 Drain the seafood and onions, reserving the marinade for brushing over kebabs during cooking.

5 Remove rind from bacon and cut lengthwise to form thin strips. Peel pawpaw or rockmelon and cut into thick chunky cubes. Thread pieces of fish, bacon, onion, pawpaw or rockmelon, and scallops or prawns onto skewers.

6 Cook under a preheated grill for 8–10 minutes, or until seafood is cooked, brushing occasionally with the marinade.

Serves 4–6

Tuna Nut Curry

425 g (14 oz) can tuna

2 fresh red chillies, seeded and finely chopped

6 spring onions or scallions, finely chopped

100 g (3⅓ oz) unsalted cashews, finely chopped

2 tspns grated lemon rind

2 tblspns oil

1⅓ cups thick Coconut Milk (see page 36)

2 tspns lemon juice

salt and pepper

1 Drain and flake tuna, set aside.

2 Mix together chillies, spring onions, cashews and lemon rind.

3 Heat oil in a heavy-based frying pan. Add chilli mixture and fry over low heat, stirring occasionally, for 5 minutes.

4 Add Coconut Milk and bring to the boil. Add tuna, mix lightly and simmer for 3 minutes or until heated through. Add lemon juice and season with salt and pepper. Serve with rice.

Serves 4

Seafood and Fruit Kebabs

CHICKEN: TENDER AND JUICY

A staple ingredient throughout India, Asia and the Pacific, chicken offers many regional flavours and styles of cooking.

Madras Chicken

1 kg (2 lb) chicken pieces

3 tblspns oil

1 onion, thinly sliced

3 dried red chillies, diced

½ tspn freshly ground black pepper

1 tspn cumin seeds

1 tspn turmeric

2 cardamom pods

440 g (14 oz) can tomatoes

2 tblspns tomato paste

2 tblspns lemon juice

1 tspn garam masala

1 Pat chicken pieces dry with absorbent paper. Heat 2 tablespoons oil in a large frying pan. Add chicken pieces and fry over moderate heat for 6–8 minutes or until golden brown. You will have to do this in a few batches.

2 Remove chicken from pan and place in a large ovenproof casserole dish.

3 If necessary, add remaining oil to frying pan and heat. Add onion, chilli and spices and fry over low heat for 4 minutes or until onion has softened slightly. Add tomatoes with their liquid and tomato paste, bring to the boil.

4 Pour over chicken, cover casserole dish with a lid and cook in a moderate oven (180ºC) for 45 minutes.

5 Remove from oven, stir in lemon juice and garam masala. Return to oven and cook for a further 20–30 minutes or until chicken is tender.

Serves 4–6

Tandoori Chicken

1 medium onion, finely chopped

1 tblspn Tandoori Mix (see page 36)

½ tspn fresh root ginger, grated

1 tblspn tomato paste

200 g natural yoghurt

1.5 kg (3 lb) chicken pieces, skin removed

paprika

1 tblspn chopped parsley

SAMBALS

stick of celery

cucumber, cut into wedges

red and green capsicum (pepper), cut into rings

1 Combine onion, Tandoori Mix, ginger and tomato paste. Add to yoghurt and mix well.

2 Coat chicken pieces well with yoghurt mixture. Place in a large, deep dish and leave chicken to marinate in refrigerator overnight.

Madras Chicken (top) and Tandoori Chicken (left), served with Melon Salad and Tomato and Mint Sambal.

3 Line an ovenproof dish with foil, place chicken and spiced yoghurt in dish. Cover to seal completely. Bake in a moderate oven (180ºC) for 45 minutes to 1 hour or until chicken is tender.

4 Unfold the foil, sprinkle lightly with paprika. Return to the oven and cook for 10 minutes or until brown. Sprinkle with parsley. Serve with sambals and rice.

Serves 6

Apricot Chicken with Rice

1.5 kg (3 lb) chicken pieces

salt and freshly ground black pepper

½ tspn cinnamon

1½ tspns curry powder

1 cup dried apricots, chopped

125 g (4 oz) butter or margarine

2 large onions, finely chopped

1 cup currants or raisins

4 cups cooked rice

¼ cup chicken stock

1 Set oven temperature at slow (150ºC). Wipe chicken pieces with absorbent paper and season with salt, pepper, cinnamon and curry powder.

2 Soak dried apricots in cold water for 5 minutes, drain.

3 Heat 60 g (2 oz) of butter or margarine in a heavy heatproof casserole and fry onions until golden, about 8 minutes. Remove and set aside.

4 Add currants or raisins and apricots to pan and cook for 5 minutes. Add to chicken.

5 Spread half the rice over base of a greased casserole dish, then pour in stock. Arrange chicken, fruit and onions over rice and top with remaining rice.

6 Dot with remaining butter or margarine, cover with a lid and cook for 45 minutes to 1 hour or until chicken is tender.

Serves 6

Chicken in Creamy Curry Sauce

⅓ cup oil

1.5 kg (3 lb) chicken pieces

3 tblspns butter or margarine

2 onions, thinly sliced

½ cup almonds

2 tspns grated fresh root ginger

3 tspns curry paste

1 tspn turmeric

½ cup raisins

2½ cups water

⅓ cup natural yoghurt

2 tblspns cream

salt and pepper

1 Heat oil in a large, heavy-based frying pan, add chicken pieces a few at a time and fry until golden brown, about 8 minutes. Remove from pan and set aside.

2 Melt butter or margarine in a large, heavy-based saucepan, add onions and fry until golden brown, about 6 minutes.

3 Add almonds, ginger, curry paste and turmeric and cook, stirring for 1 minute. Gradually stir in raisins and water, return chicken to pan, cover with a lid and simmer for 25 minutes.

4 Remove lid and simmer without a lid for 15 minutes or until sauce has thickened slightly and chicken is tender.

5 Remove pan from heat and stir in yoghurt and cream, reheat gently, do not boil. Season to taste with salt and pepper if necessary and serve hot.

Serves 4–6

Shakuti

size 15 (3 lb) chicken

3 tblspns ghee

2 tspns ground cumin

2 tspns ground coriander

2 whole cloves

1 tspn freshly ground black pepper

1 tspn paprika

1 tspn turmeric

½ tspn ground nutmeg

3 cloves garlic, chopped

2 onions, chopped

1 tblspn tomato paste

1 cup thick Coconut Milk (see page 36)

1 cup chicken stock

¼ cup desiccated coconut

1 Cut chicken into serving pieces, pat dry with absorbent paper. Heat ghee in large frying pan, add chicken and fry until golden brown, about 6–8 minutes. Remove from pan and drain on absorbent paper.

2 Add spices, garlic and onion and fry until onion has softened, about 6–8 minutes. Stir in tomato paste and cook for 1 minute.

3 Add chicken, Coconut Milk, stock and desiccated coconut, mix well and bring to the boil.

4 Cover pan with a lid, lower heat and simmer for 40 minutes or until chicken is almost tender.

5 Remove lid from pan and simmer for a further 10 minutes or until sauce is thick and dry.

Serves 4–6

Curried Roast Poussin

4 x 400 g (12 oz) poussin or spatchcock

1 tblspn butter or margarine

STUFFING

1 tblspn butter or margarine

1 onion, finely chopped

2 tspns curry powder

¾ cup cooked brown rice

2 tblspns finely chopped parsley

1 hard-boiled egg, peeled and chopped

salt and pepper to taste

1 Melt butter or margarine in a heavy-based frying pan, add onion and fry until onion has softened, about 5 minutes.

2 Add curry powder and fry, stirring all the time for a further 1 minute. Remove pan from heat.

3 Place rice, parsley, egg and seasonings in a mixing bowl, add fried onion mixture and stir until ingredients are well combined.

4 Wash birds and pat dry with absorbent paper. Fill with the stuffing and close cavity with a skewer or tie with string. Tie legs together with string.

5 Place the birds on a rack and stand in a baking dish. Using fingertips, rub them all over with butter or margarine.

6 Bake in a moderate oven (180°C) for 45 minutes, or until the juices run clear when each bird is pierced with a skewer and skin is golden brown.

7 Spoon pan juices over the bird as it cooks – this will help to brown the skin. Remove from baking dish, take out skewer and string.

Serves 6

Curried Roast Poussin

Grilled Spiced Chicken

size 15 (3 lb) chicken

salt and freshly ground black pepper

1 tblspn ground coriander

½ tspn chilli powder

¼ tspn ground ginger

½ tspn turmeric

60 g (2 oz) butter or margarine

1 tblspn lemon juice

1 Remove neck and giblets from chicken, if necessary. Cut into serving pieces and wipe dry with absorbent paper. Rub chicken pieces well with salt and pepper.

2 Place spices, butter or margarine and lemon juice in a small saucepan and melt over very low heat.

3 Place chicken on griller rack in preheated grill. Brush with butter mixture.

4 Grill skin side down for about 15 minutes, brushing several times with butter mixture.

5 Turn chicken, continue to brush and cook for a further 15 minutes or until chicken is tender and brown.

Serves 4–6

Curry Baked Chicken

2 kg (4 lb) chicken maryland pieces

MARINADE

1 cup natural yoghurt

½ cup tomato puree

3 cloves garlic, crushed

1 tblspn lemon juice

2 tspns curry paste

1 tblspn brown sugar

paprika for sprinkling

1 Wash chicken pieces and pat dry with absorbent paper. Make small slits all over surface of chicken using a small sharp knife.

2 Place all marinade ingredients in a large bowl and mix well. Spread marinade all over chicken, pushing it into slits.

3 Place chicken and remaining marinade in a large dish, cover with plastic wrap and chill overnight.

4 Place chicken pieces skin side up in a large baking dish. Bake in a very hot oven (220ºC) for 15 minutes.

5 Lower heat to moderate (180ºC) and cook for a further 30 minutes or until chicken is tender and skin is crisp.

Serves 8

Peanut Chicken

1 kg (2 lb) chicken pieces

1 clove garlic, crushed

pinch salt

1 tblspn vinegar

1 tspn ground cumin

½ cup crunchy peanut butter

1 tblspn sugar

1 tspn soy sauce

¼ cup milk

¼ cup chicken stock

bay leaf

1 Wipe chicken with absorbent paper.

2 Combine garlic with remaining ingredients in a large bowl. Add chicken and toss thoroughly to coat each piece. Cover and marinate for at least 1 hour or overnight.

3 Arrange chicken pieces in a single layer in a roasting tin. Cook in a moderate oven (180ºC) for 45 minutes or until chicken is tender. Brush frequently with marinade during cooking. Serve with boiled rice and remaining marinade.

Serves 4–6

THE SAVOURY TASTE OF BEEF

Spicy meat dishes vary as much as the regions from which they originate. This selection reflects that variety – mild and hot, old and new.

Curried Beef and Lentils

250g (8oz) yellow or red lentils, washed

250g (8oz) chick peas, soaked overnight and drained

1kg (2lb) chuck (or stewing) steak, cut into small cubes

2 large potatoes, peeled and cut into cubes

2 cloves garlic, crushed

1 onion, finely chopped

½ bunch spinach (approximately 5 leaves), washed and finely shredded

2 tblspns chopped mint

2 tblspns chopped parsley

1 tblspn curry powder

5 cups water

salt to taste

1 Place all ingredients except salt in a large saucepan. Stir well and bring to the boil.

2 Lower heat, cover pan with a lid and simmer for 1½ hours or until meat is tender. Season to taste with salt.

Serves 8–10

Malayan Beef Sate

750g (1½lb) rump steak, cut into 2cm (1in) cubes

¼ cup soy sauce

¼ cup oil

2 onions, finely chopped

2 cloves garlic, crushed

2 tspns ground cumin

1 tspn lemon juice

salt and pepper

1 Place steak cubes in an earthenware bowl and add soy sauce, oil, onions and garlic. Marinate for 3 hours then drain, reserving the marinade.

2 Thread steak cubes onto small wooden skewers and brush with a mixture of ground cumin and lemon juice.

3 Grill over barbecue or under hot grill, brushing meat with marinade and turning skewers from time to time. Cook for 10 minutes or until meat is tender. Season with salt and pepper and serve.

Serves 6

Curried Beef and Lentils

Meat and Vegetable Curry

750g (1½ lb) chuck or stewing steak

½ cup natural yoghurt

1 tblspn curry paste

2 tblspns ghee or oil

2 onions, thinly sliced

2 cloves garlic, crushed

1 tspn garam masala

2 potatoes, peeled and diced

2 carrots, peeled and diced

250g (8 oz) green beans, cut into pieces

salt to taste

1 Trim excess fat from meat and cut into 2cm (1 in) cubes. Mix together yoghurt and curry paste and place in a bowl with meat. Mix well and leave for 2 hours.

2 Heat ghee in a large saucepan or heatproof casserole and fry onion and garlic until softened, about 4 minutes.

3 Add meat and yoghurt mixture, cover pan with a lid and simmer for 1 hour.

4 Add garam masala, vegetables and salt to taste. Mix well and simmer for a further 30 minutes or until meat and vegetables are tender.

Serves 4

Kofta Curry

MEATBALLS

500g (1 lb) mince or ground beef

1 large potato, cooked and mashed

1 onion, finely chopped

½ green pepper, seeded and finely chopped

2 cloves garlic, crushed

1 tspn chilli powder

2 tspns garam masala

1 egg, lightly beaten

salt and pepper to taste

SAUCE

2 tblspns ghee or oil

2 onions, finely chopped

2 cloves garlic, crushed

1 tspn garam masala

440g (14 oz) can peeled tomatoes, chopped

1 Place all meatball ingredients in a large bowl and mix until well combined. Shape mixture into 3cm (1¼ in) balls and set aside.

2 Heat ghee or oil in a large, heavy-based saucepan, add onions and garlic and fry over moderate heat until onions have softened and are golden, about 8 minutes.

3 Add garam masala and cook, stirring for a further minute.

4 Stir in tomatoes with their liquid and bring to the boil.

5 Carefully add meatballs, lower heat and simmer without a lid until meatballs are tender and sauce is thick, about 20–25 minutes. Stir occasionally during cooking, being careful not to break the meatballs. If sauce becomes too thick, add a little extra water.

Serves 4

Madras Beef Curry

60g (2 oz) ghee

3 onions, chopped

3 cloves garlic, crushed

6 tspns curry powder

1.5kg (3 lb) chuck or stewing steak, cut into 2cm (1 in) cubes

2 tspns salt

1½ cups thick Coconut Milk (see page 36)

440g (14 oz) can tomatoes

1 Heat ghee in a large, heavy-based saucepan. Add onion and garlic and fry until golden brown, about 8 minutes.

Meat and Vegetable Curry (right) and Kofta Curry (left).

2 Add curry powder and cook for 2–3 minutes. Add meat and mix until meat is well coated with spice mixture. Stir in remaining ingredients and bring to the boil.

3 Lower heat, cover pan with a lid and simmer for 1½–2 hours or until meat is tender.

Serves 8

Beef and Broccoli

2 tblspns oil
1 clove garlic, crushed
2 tspns grated fresh root ginger
750 g (1½ lb) round or rump steak, sliced into thin strips
¾ cup cashews
2 tblspns soy sauce
2 tspns brown sugar
1 chicken stock cube
¾ cup water
2 tspns curry paste
1 tblspn sweet sherry
375 g (12 oz) broccoli florets
1 red capsicum (red pepper), seeded and cut into cubes
2 tspns cornflour
extra ½ cup water

1 Heat oil in a large, heavy-based frying pan. Add garlic and ginger and fry until golden, about 2–3 minutes.

2 Add strips of meat and cashews and fry over very high heat until meat is almost tender and cashews are golden brown. Remove meat and cashews from pan and drain on absorbent paper.

3 Mix together soy sauce, brown sugar, crumbled stock cube, water, curry paste and sherry and pour into pan. Add broccoli and capsicum and cook for 1–2 minutes.

4 Mix cornflour with extra water. Pour into pan. Bring sauce to the boil, stirring all the time.

5 Lower heat, return meat and cashews to pan and simmer for 2 minutes or until meat is coated with sauce and heated through.

Serves 4–6

Spiced Kebabs

1 kg (2 lb) topside or stewing steak
4 small onions
5 cm (2 in) piece fresh root ginger
2 tblspns vinegar
½ tspn chilli powder
½ tspn ground turmeric
1 tspn ground coriander
1 tspn ground cumin
1 cup beef stock
½ cup natural yoghurt
1 tblspn cornflour

1 Cut meat into 2 cm (1 in) cubes. Peel onions, cut into quarters, then separate into segments. Thinly slice ginger.

2 Thread meat, onion and ginger alternately onto 8 skewers.

3 Place vinegar and spices in a heavy-based, shallow frying pan and cook paste over gentle heat for 1–2 minutes, taking care not to burn it.

4 Stir in stock. Add skewers to pan and cover frying pan tightly with a lid. Bring to boil, then lower heat and simmer gently for 45 minutes, or until meat is tender. Remove kebabs from pan and keep warm.

5 Mix yoghurt and cornflour in a small bowl. Stir in 2 tablespoons cooking liquid and mix until smooth. Stir yoghurt mixture into sauce and bring slowly to the boil, whisking constantly.

6 Serve kebabs with rice. Serve sauce separately.

Serves 4

Beef and Broccoli

Chilli Ground Beef

2 tblspns oil

2 onions, finely chopped

2 cloves garlic, crushed

2 tspns grated fresh root ginger

750g (1½ lb) mince or ground beef

1 cup beef stock

½ cup tomato paste

1 red pepper, seeded and cut into thin strips

½ tspn chilli powder

salt and pepper to taste

3 tspns garam masala

1 Heat oil in a heavy-based saucepan. Add onion, garlic and ginger and fry over moderate heat until onion softens, about 5 minutes.

2 Add ground beef and fry over moderately high heat, pressing down with a fork until meat is well browned and crumbly.

3 Add stock, tomato paste, red pepper and chilli powder, mix well and season to taste with salt and pepper. Bring to the boil, then lower heat and simmer for 1 hour or until almost all liquid has been absorbed.

4 Stir in garam masala and cook for a further 2 minutes.

Serves 4–6

Beef Vindaloo

3kg (6lb) chuck or stewing steak

MARINADE

1½ cups malt vinegar

1½ cups water

6 tspns grated fresh root ginger

6 cloves garlic, crushed

10 small dried chillies, crushed

3 tspns ground cumin

1 tspn ground cloves

1 tspn ground cardamom

6 cinnamon sticks

1 tspn nutmeg

6 tspns salt

1 tspn freshly ground black pepper

TO FINISH

½ cup oil

6 onions, finely chopped

1 Trim any excess fat and gristle from beef and cut into large cubes.

2 Combine all marinade ingredients in a large bowl, add beef and mix well. Cover with plastic wrap and chill for 4 hours.

3 Heat oil in a large, heavy-based saucepan, add onions and fry for 8–10 minutes or until onions have softened slightly.

4 Add meat and marinade, bring to the boil, lower heat and simmer covered with a lid for 2 hours or until beef is tender, stirring occasionally.

Serves 10–12

Crisp Fried Beef

750g (1½ lb) round or stewing steak

1 large onion, diced

2 tspns sugar

3 tspns coriander seeds, ground

2 tspns cumin seeds, ground

1 tspn grated fresh root ginger

½ tspn peppercorns, crushed

2 tspns vinegar

100g (4oz) ground peanuts

¼ cup Chilli Sauce (see page 36)

1 Cut beef into thin slices, about 6cm (2½ in) long.

2 Mix all remaining ingredients together to a coarse paste. Coat beef well with paste.

3 Place meat in a single layer in a lightly greased baking dish and cook in a moderate oven (180ºC) for 1 hour or until meat is dry, crisp and tender.

Serves 4

Meatballs with Yoghurt Sauce

MEATBALLS

1 cup desiccated coconut

3 tblspns water

1 tspn curry powder

500g (1lb) mince or ground beef

1 onion, finely chopped

1 clove garlic, crushed

1 egg

1 tblspn natural yoghurt

½ tspn ground coriander

½ tspn ground cumin

¼ tspn ground ginger

salt and freshly ground pepper to taste

oil for frying

YOGHURT SAUCE

½ cup natural yoghurt

2 tspns lemon juice

1 tspn curry powder

2 tspns fruit chutney

1 Place all yoghurt sauce ingredients in a small saucepan and heat gently.

2 Place desiccated coconut and 3 tablespoons water in a small bowl. Mix well and leave to soak for 5 minutes.

3 Place remaining meatball ingredients, except oil, in a bowl and mix until well combined. Stir in coconut mixture.

4 Pinch off pieces of meat mixture and shape into meatballs.

5 Heat oil in a deep, heavy-based saucepan or deep fryer and fry meatballs until golden brown, about 3–5 minutes.

6 Drain on absorbent paper and serve with Yoghurt Sauce.

Serves 4

Chilli Ground Beef

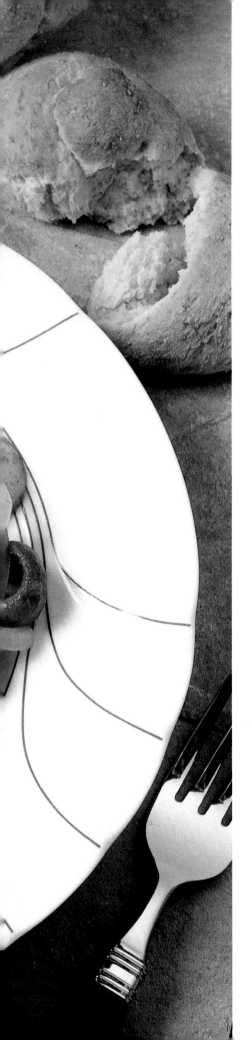

PORK: A VARIABLE FEAST

From spicy Pork Vindaloo to the sweet taste of Honey Pork, there's an abundance of reasons for trying new ways with this tender meat.

Pork Vindaloo

1 kg (2 lb) pork shoulder

MARINADE

4 large onions, finely chopped

4 cloves garlic, crushed

6 tspns garam masala

2 tspns chopped fresh chilli

1 tspn freshly ground black pepper

1 tspn salt

1 cup malt vinegar

1 tblspn brown sugar

1 tblspn ghee or oil

1 Trim excess fat or sinew from pork and cut into 2 cm (1 in) cubes.

2 Place all marinade ingredients except ghee or oil in a large glass or china bowl. Add pork and mix until ingredients are well combined. Cover with plastic wrap and refrigerate overnight.

3 Strain marinade liquid from pork and set aside.

4 Heat ghee or oil in a large, heavy-based saucepan, add pork and onion mixture and cook, tossing all the time over high heat until pork changes colour, about 5 minutes.

5 Add reserved marinade liquid and bring to the boil. Lower heat, cover pan with lid and simmer gently for 1 hour.

6 Remove lid and simmer for a further 30 minutes, or until pork is tender.

Serves 6

Chilli Marinated Spare Ribs

1.5 kg (3 lb) pork spare ribs

1 tspn salt

1 tspn mixed spice

1½ tspns brown sugar

½ tspn chilli powder

2 tspns dry sherry

1 tblspn tomato sauce (catsup)

2 tspns honey

¼ cup stock

1 Slash the rind of the spare ribs at 1 cm (½ in) intervals, cutting through the rind but not through the meat.

2 Mix the salt, mixed spice, sugar, chilli, sherry, tomato sauce (catsup) and honey together.

3 Place the spare ribs in a large shallow dish, pour over the sauce mixture and leave to stand for at least 2 hours, preferably overnight.

Pork Vindaloo with tomato and mushroom accompaniment

4 Using a slotted spoon, remove the pork from the marinade and put the marinade to one side.

5 Place the ribs on a roasting rack and stand over a baking dish containing about 1 cm (½ in) of water. Roast in a moderately hot oven (190°C) for 1¼ hours or until tender and golden brown. Brush every now and then with the marinade and turn several times.

6 To serve, cut spare ribs into pieces. Pour the remaining marinade into a small saucepan. Add stock, bring to the boil, then lower the heat and simmer for a few minutes. Pour over the pork and serve.

Serves 4–6

Curried Pork Sausages

500 g (1 lb) fatty pork, cut into cubes

4 slices bread, crusts removed

1 large onion, peeled and quartered

2 eggs

1½ tspns curry powder

¼ tspn ground pepper

½ tspn cumin

½ tspn salt

sausage casings

Note: Natural sausage casings are available from good butchers. Ask your butcher to order them for you if necessary. This recipe uses a pasta and sausage-maker attachment on a food processor (you can also use a large piping bag fitted with a large nozzle) to firmly extrude the sausage mixture into the moist casings, twisting as each sausage is formed.

1 Remove any sinew and gristle from meat. Using a food processor or electric blender, process meat, bread and onion together until finely minced but not smooth. You may have to do this in several batches.

2 Place in a mixing bowl. Add all other ingredients, except sausage casings, and mix well.

3 Place sausage casings in a bowl of cold water and untangle. Push end of casings over tap nozzle and turn on tap gently to fill casing with water.

4 Gently push one end of the casing over the sausage nozzle attachment and place in position on the machine. Push sausage mixture down the barrel and place food guide in position.

5 Switch on machine until sausage mixture begins to enter sausage nozzle. Switch off machine and tie a knot in the end of casing. Turn on machine again and allow sausage mixture to extrude.

6 When desired sausage length is obtained, pinch and twist sausage to separate and continue processing until all mixture is used. Place a slice of bread in barrel to push remaining mixture out of nozzle.

7 Once made, the sausage mixture should be used the same day or frozen immediately. When cooking, pierce skins with a fork to prevent sausages bursting and barbecue, grill, fry or cook as liked.

Makes 700 g (1½ lb) of sausages

Spicy Honey Pork

3 tblspns oil

500 g (1 lb) pork fillet, cut into 2.5 cm (1 in) strips

½ cup chopped spring onions (scallions)

1 clove garlic, crushed

3 cups grated carrot

½ tspn chilli powder

1½ cups chicken stock

¼ cup white wine

⅓ cup honey

salt and pepper to taste

1 Heat oil in a heavy-based saucepan. Add pork strips, about 6 at a time, and fry quickly over high heat,

Curried Pork Sausages

tossing until pork is crisp and golden brown, about 3–4 minutes for each batch. Remove pork from the pan when cooked and drain on absorbent paper.

2 Add scallions, garlic, carrot and chilli powder to pan and fry quickly, stirring, for 5–6 minutes, or until vegetables have softened.

3 Mix together stock, wine and honey. Pour over vegetables in pan and bring to the boil, stirring all the time.

4 Lower heat and simmer for 15 minutes, or until liquid reduces by half.

5 Add pork strips and simmer for a further 5 minutes or until pork is heated through. Season to taste with salt and pepper. Serve with fluffy boiled rice.

Serves 4

Chilli Pork

2 tblspns oil

750 g (1½ lb) pork schnitzels

4 onions, thinly sliced

2 cloves garlic, crushed

½ tspn chilli powder

1 tblspn tomato sauce

2 tspns soy sauce

½ tspn allspice

2 tspns brown sugar

1 tblspn vinegar

1 Heat oil in a large frying pan. Add pork schnitzels and fry until brown on both sides, about 3–4 minutes. Remove from pan.

2 Add onion and garlic to pan and cook until onion has softened slightly, about 4 minutes.

Chilli Pork

3 Add chilli powder and cook, stirring constantly, for 2 minutes.

4 Return meat to pan.

5 Mix remaining ingredients together and pour over meat. Cook for a further 3 minutes or until meat is tender.

Serves 4

(Continued page 41)

QUICK REFERENCE

G U I D E

All the information you need on
Oven Temperatures
Measurement Equivalents
Storing/Freezing Methods
Common Cooking Terms and Hints
Herb Guide
Marinades That Work

SPECIAL SECTION
SECRETS OF SPICY FOOD SUCCESS

MAKING A GOOD START

The difference between a real curry and a westernised version lies in basic ingredients and cooking techniques. Here we show how to achieve an authentic flavour.

THE RIGHT INGREDIENTS

ALLSPICE

A West Indian spice resembling in flavour a combination of nutmeg, mace and cinnamon.

ATTA

A fine wholemeal flour used to make Indian breads. If unavailable, substitute fine wholemeal flour which can be bought at health food stores.

BASIL

A sweet, pungent herb available fresh, dried or ground. Used frequently in Indonesian dishes.

BESAN

A yellow flour made from channa (chick peas). Available from Asian food stores and health food stores. If unavailable, substitute finely sifted pea flour.

BLACHAN

Dried shrimp paste. A strongly flavoured paste made from fermented prawns. Sold in cans or cakes, this paste can be stored in an airtight container in the pantry.

BOMBAY DUCK

A type of salted dried fish, which can be served as an accompaniment to a curry meal or used as a flavouring. Sold in packets, Bombay duck should be cut into pieces no larger than 2.5 cm (1 in) then deep fried or grilled to serve as a side dish, or it can be ground and used to season sauces.

CARDAMOM

This fragrant spice is native to India and is a member of the ginger family. Creamy pods contain two clusters of seeds which have an aromatic, sweet and haunting flavour.

CARAWAY SEEDS

Small, brown crescent-shaped seeds with a strong, distinctive flavour. Use sparingly.

CASHEWS

Sweet, kidney-shaped nuts from the cashew tree. Available raw from many supermarkets and health food stores.

CHANNA

Creamy-yellow dried peas also known as chick peas. Used extensively in Indian cooking.

CHILLIES

Fresh: Red or green chillies are available from most greengrocers. They vary in size and degree of hotness and can be used whole or finely chopped as a flavouring in curries and sambals. The seeds are the hottest part so, if you wish, you can remove them before using the rest of the chilli. When preparing chillies for cooking, wear rubber gloves to avoid burning your skin.
Dried: Available from supermarkets in packets. These are usually fresh red chillies which have been dried. They should be soaked in hot water for 20 minutes before using, unless recipe states otherwise.
Powder: The powder obtained by grinding dried red chillies.
Sauce: Malaysian or Singaporean chilli sauce is a hot sauce made from red chillies, ginger, garlic and flavourings, often sweetened with fruit.

CINNAMON

Available ground or in stick form. Cinnamon sticks can be kept for a longer period of time than ground cinnamon. Use to flavour sweet and savoury dishes.

CLOVES

The dried flower buds of a tree native to South-East Asia. Available whole or ground, cloves have a strong flavour and should be used subtly.

COCONUT MILK

The liquid extracted from the grated white flesh of fresh coconuts, or desiccated coconut. Coconut milk can also be bought in cans or as compressed cakes, which should be diluted with warm water to obtain the desired consistency.

CORIANDER

Fresh: Also called Chinese parsley, fresh coriander has a distinctive flavour.
Dried: A small, round dried seed, coriander is the main spice in curry powder.

CUMIN

Black: A peppery, aromatic spice used in some Indian dishes.

White: Similar to caraway seeds in shape. Sold whole or ground, cumin seeds have a sweet flavour. An important ingredient in garam masala and prepared curry powder.

CURRY LEAVES

Small dried leaves used in curries and other Indian and Malaysian dishes. Available from Asian and health food stores.

CURRY PASTE

A paste made from a mixture of spices cooked with oil or coconut milk. Available commercially or can be prepared at home.

CURRY POWDER

Available commercially, however in countries where curry is eaten daily, spices are always freshly ground.

FENNEL

Often called large cumin, fennel has a sweet taste and fragrance. Available in seed form or ground.

FENUGREEK

Small, square, brownish-coloured seeds with a bitter flavour, fenugreek is often used in fish curries.

GARAM MASALA

A blend of ground spices used in Indian cooking. The combination of spices can vary.

GARLIC

An essential flavouring ingredient in Asian cooking. Garlic can vary in colour and size.

GHEE

Clarified butter. It can be heated to a high temperature without burning and is the main cooking medium in Northern India. Available at supermarkets and Asian stores.

GINGER

Fresh ginger is an indispensable ingredient in all Asian cooking. Before using, remove skin with a sharp knife and slice, shred, chop or grate, according to recipe instructions. Powdered ginger should not be substituted for fresh as the flavour is different.

LEMON GRASS

Native to Asia, the white, bulbous part of the grass is used to impart a lemony flavour and fragrance to Asian dishes. Also available dried. You will need to substitute approximately 12 strips dried lemon grass for 1 fresh stem.

LENTILS

Dried peas and beans widely used in Indian cooking. Lentils are a good source of protein and can be used to make soups, sauces, vegetarian meals or savouries. They can also be added to meat or poultry curries.

LIME

Juice is added to curry meals to give a sharp, piquant flavour. Lemon juice can be substituted.

MACE

Part of the nutmeg, but with a more delicate flavour.

MALDIVE FISH

Dried tuna. It is sold in packets and should be crushed before using. Widely used in Sri Lankan cooking.

MINT

There are many varieties of this fresh-tasting, green herb. However, the round-leafed mint is generally used to flavour curries.

MUSTARD SEEDS

Black mustard seeds are small, dark seeds with a pungent flavour used in Indian cooking.

NUTMEG

A firm nut usually sold in its shell. For best flavour, grate or pound to a powder when ready to use. Mostly used in cakes and sweets.

ONION

A bulbous plant root used to add flavour to most dishes. Two common varieties are white and brown. Brown onions have a stronger flavour.

PAPPADAMS

Thin lentil and spice wafers available in packets from Asian food stores and some supermarkets. Serve as an accompaniment to curries.

PAPRIKA

Dried and ground paprika peppers should have a strong red colour and mild, sweet flavour.

PEPPER

Black: The sun-dried berry from a vine. A vital ingredient of garam masala.
White: Comes from the same vine as the black pepper, but the ripe berries are immersed in water until the outer skin rots, leaving the white seed. These seeds are then dried.

PEPPERS

(Or capsicum.) Red and green in colour, they have a mild, sweet flavour and are used as a vegetable or salad ingredient.

POPPY SEEDS

(White.) When ground, these seeds are used for thickening sauces, gravies, etc.

ROSEWATER

A delicate essence of roses, mostly used to flavour Indian sweets and cakes. It differs from rose essence which is concentrated. Available from Asian food stores.

SAFFRON

An expensive spice with a strong perfume. The orange-coloured threads give a bright yellow colour and marvellous flavour to many Indian meals, especially rice dishes. Turmeric can be used to give the same colour but it lacks flavour.

SAMBAL BAJAK

A compound mixture of chillies and spices used as an accompaniment to curry. Sold at specialty Asian stores and some delicatessens.

SESAME SEEDS

Tiny oval seeds high in protein with a nutty taste. Used as a garnish in sweets or ground for use in savoury dishes. Often toasted to increase the flavour.

SOY SAUCE

Made from salted soy beans, this is a common sauce used extensively in Asian cooking. The three different grades are light, dark and sweet. Kecap Maris is the name given to Indonesian soy sauce which is thick, dark and sweet.

SPRING ONIONS

(Scallions.) White, slender bulbs with a green leaf top and a delicate onion flavour, they are a member of the onion family.

TAMARIND

The fruit from the tamarind tree. Tamarind adds a slight flavour and strong acidity to dishes. It is sold dried in packets and must be reconstituted before using. To reconstitute, soak a small piece in half-cup hot water for 10 minutes, then squeeze to extract liquid and mix with water. If unavailable substitute vinegar, lime or lemon juice.

TURMERIC

Usually sold powdered, turmeric is used for seasoning and colouring curry dishes. It is bright yellow in colour with a slightly bitter taste.

YOGHURT

Natural unflavoured yoghurt is widely used in Indian cooking as a salad dressing, in sauces, to tenderise meats, as a side dish or for thickening.

THE AUTHENTIC TOUCH

SPICES

The selective and imaginative use of spices is important when creating curry-style dishes. The combination of spices used gives each dish its individual and distinctive flavour.

In countries where curry dishes are eaten daily, commercial curry powders and pastes are not used. Instead, whole fresh spices are ground just before using for optimum flavour.

Traditionally spices were ground with a grinding stone and pestle, however a small electric spice or coffee grinder gives excellent results.

Buy spices in small quantities and store in airtight containers in a cool, dark cupboard. Whole spices keep better than ground. They will store successfully for up to 1 year. Ground spices will store for 3 months.

TANDOORI MIX

1 tblspn paprika
1 tblspn coriander seeds, ground
1 tblspn cumin seeds, ground
3 tspns ground ginger
1 tspn turmeric

Mix all ingredients together and use as required.
Makes approximately ⅓ cup

CHILLI SAUCE

6 fresh red chillies, seeded and diced
1 tspn chilli powder
3 cups sugar
1½ cups vinegar
2 tspns ground cumin
4 cloves garlic, crushed
2 tspns grated fresh root ginger
1 tblspn tomato paste
250 g (8 oz) sultanas

Place all ingredients in a large enamel or stainless steel saucepan and bring to the boil. Lower heat and simmer until sultanas are very soft, about 30–40 minutes. Cool, then pour into electric blender or food processor and process until pureed. Pour into warm sterilised bottles, seal, label and store in a cool dry place.
Makes approximately 3 cups

COCONUT MILK

Coconut milk is an important ingredient used in many curries. It is the liquid extracted from the grated white flesh of coconuts or desiccated coconut.

There are two types of coconut milk – thick coconut milk, which results from the first squeezing of the grated or desiccated coconut, and thin coconut milk which is made from the second squeezing of the coconut.

Use a combination of both extracts in recipes requiring coconut milk unless thick or thin coconut milk is specified.

2½ cups water
2 cups desiccated coconut
salt

Place water and coconut in a saucepan and heat gently but do not boil. Cool to lukewarm then pour half into an electric blender or food processor and process for a few seconds or knead well to extract flavour from coconut. Repeat with remaining liquid. Strain through cheesecloth and squeeze to extract richness. Repeat process using same coconut and another 2½ cups hot water. Combine with first infusion. Add a small pinch of salt. Store in the refrigerator until ready to use.
Makes 2½ cups

CURRY POWDER

Making your own curry powder is easy to do and results in a flavoursome mix. It is best to make it in small quantities to ensure freshness, so you can halve this recipe.

60 g (2 oz) ground turmeric
60 g (2 oz) coriander seeds
60 g (2 oz) cumin seeds
15 g (½ oz) chilli powder
15 g (½ oz) fennel seeds
15 g (½ oz) fenugreek seeds
30 g (1 oz) ground ginger
7 g (¼ oz) yellow mustard seeds

Grind spices to a powder in an electric blender or with a mortar and pestle. Place all ingredients in a large bowl and mix until well combined. Place prepared curry mixture in a bottle or tin, and seal firmly with a lid. Curry powder can be stored on the shelf for up to 2 months.
Makes 2½ cups

COMMON COOKING TERMS AND HANDY HINTS

Bain-marie A shallow pan of warm or simmering water in which another dish is placed, providing a gentle, smooth way of cooking or heating.

Baste To spoon liquid, stock, melted butter or fat over foods while cooking.

Beat To mix foods thoroughly with a spoon or whisk. A hand-held electric beater saves time and effort.

Blanch To plunge food into boiling water to partially or fully cook. Blanching also removes strong taste of onions or cabbage and removes the salty, smoky taste of bacon.

Blanched almonds Method of removing skins by dropping almonds into boiling water, then slipping skins off with the fingers while the almonds are still warm.

Blend To mix foods gently with a fork, spoon or spatula.

Boil There are slow, medium and fast boils. A very slow boil where the water is hardly moving is a simmer.

Breadcrumbs Make your own by using stale bread or bread you have hardened in a slow oven. Place the bread in an electric blender and keep the crumbs in an airtight jar.

Braise To brown food in fat or butter before cooking in a covered pot with a small amount of liquid.

Broil The word used in America for 'grill'.

Burns Soothe a minor burn by rubbing with the cut surface of a raw potato.

Coffee To sharpen the flavour of coffee, add a tiny pinch of salt as you pour boiling water over the ground coffee.

Cream To whip cream use a clean whisk or beater in a chilled bowl, preferably metal.

Croutons Small squares of stale bread tossed in butter or oil. Brown on both sides and use as a garnish for soups, etc.

Degreasing To remove extra fat from a soup, stew or sauce, chill the dish and remove fat when cold. If there is not enough time, let the liquid cool slightly, tip the pot and spoon off the fat. Absorbent paper can be used if necessary to soak up any remaining fat from the surface.

Dice To cut food into small cubes, approximately 3mm (⅛ in) square.

Fat When melting fat, add a little cold water.

Gratine To brown the top of a dish under a hot griller. Sprinkle breadcrumbs, grated cheese and dots of butter to form a nice brown crust.

Lemon juice Cut lemon in half, wrap in the corner of a tea-towel and squeeze out the juice without pips.

Meat To carve roasted or braised meat, allow to rest for around 15 minutes covered with foil. You'll find it easier to carve.

Marinate To place foods in a liquid so that they will absorb flavour or become more tender.

Mince To chop very finely.

Orange peel Usually only the coloured peel – the zest – is used because the white part is bitter. Use a vegetable peeler or small grater. Peel (including the white part) left to dry for several months loses its bitterness.

Puree To mash food to a thick paste, as with mashed potatoes or apple sauce.

Pepper Always grind freshly and add at the end of cooking for best taste.

Reduce To boil down a liquid, reducing it in quantity and strengthening its taste.

Saute To cook and brown food in a small quantity of hot fat or butter. Always make sure the fat is very hot, the food is dry and the pan is not overcrowded. If necessary, saute food in small batches.

Tomatoes To peel, seed and juice, drop tomatoes one at a time into boiling water for 10 seconds. Plunge immediately into cold water, then remove skin by hand. Cut in half and squeeze gently to seed and juice.

KNOW YOUR HERBS

Angelica Most often used as a candied stem for decorating puddings and cakes. Use fresh with rhubarb and jams.

Basil A natural with tomatoes in a salad, as well as with eggplant (aubergine), zucchini (courgettes) and marrow. Pesto, a combination of basil and pine nuts, is one of the world's great tastes.

Bay These leaves and twigs are used in fish stocks, broths, stews, sauces and marinades. Keep a supply of dried leaves, but throw them out after a year or so as they do eventually lose their flavour.

Bouquet garni Usually a few sprigs of parsley, thyme and a bay leaf tied with cotton. Also available in sachets from your supermarket or delicatessen. Used in soups and stews and discarded after cooking.

Chervil This herb has a delicate flavour of aniseed and should be used generously. Use in salads, with eggs, with steaks or fish.

Chives Finer than onions, chives are used in omelettes, with tomatoes and, together with cream, on baked potatoes.

Coriander *Adds a superb flavour to meatballs and lamb stews, and features often in Chinese and Thai dishes. Essential in many curry recipes.*

Dill *Use with boiled or mashed potatoes and with any kind of white fish. Freezes well in a plastic bag.*

Fennel *The aniseed flavour of fennel goes well with most seafood. Also delicious with beans, pork or lamb.*

Fines Herbes *Chopped mixture of parsley, chervil, chives and sometimes tarragon. Used for flavouring delicate dishes such as eggs and poached fish.*

Lovage *Use sparingly in stocks and soups with a meaty flavour.*

Marjoram *Fresh leaves are used in a salad or on lamb kebabs, with tomatoes in stews or casseroles, or with lamb, chicken or game.*

Mint *Best known as an accompaniment to lamb. Use also with new potatoes, garden peas, fresh orange desserts and grilled shellfish.*

Oregano *Dried leaves add to the flavour of fish and roasts, as well as featuring in pizzas and spaghetti sauce. Sensational with mozzarella and tomatoes.*

Parsley *Flat-leafed parsley is tastier than the curled variety, but any form of this popular herb will enliven most dishes. Easy to grow in your herb garden or on the window-sill.*

Rosemary *Use with veal, lamb, pork or rabbit, or in the butter when you fry onions or potatoes.*

Sage *Use in stuffings for roast pork, goose, pork pies and sausages.*

Tarragon *Delightful summer herb that enhances the flavour of all egg dishes, chicken, ham, green salads, cold salmon and trout.*

Thyme *An attractive element in any long-simmered and red-wine dish. Use, together with tomatoes, in rabbit, chicken and veal dishes.*

MARINADES

A marinade is a seasoned liquid in which foods (mainly meat and fish) are steeped. This seasons the food by impregnating it with the flavours of the herbs and spices used. The length of time the food should be left in the marinade depends on its size and texture.

In winter, large cuts of meat can be marinated for five or six days. In summer, they should be marinated for no longer than 24 hours or, if they are placed in the refrigerator, allow 48 hours.

Marinating softens the fibres of some kinds of meat and enables it to keep longer.

Wine Marinade

This marinade is suitable for any meat. When marinating red meats, use red wine. Use whites for white meats.

1 cup wine
4 tblspns olive oil
4 parsley sprigs
2 thyme sprigs or ½ tspn of dried thyme
1 tblspn brandy
1 tspn peppercorns
1 bay leaf
3 whole cloves
1 onion, sliced
1 carrot, sliced
2 garlic cloves, peeled and cut in half

Place the meat in a glass or enamel container. Add all other ingredients, cover and chill several hours or overnight. Sufficient for 1–1.5 kg (2–3 lb) of meat.

Note: For large joints to be roasted or pot roasted, increase wine by 2 cups. It is preferable to use olive oil for marinades because of its fruity flavour.

Lamb or Beef

1 cup red wine
¼ cup wine vinegar
2 tblspns olive oil
12 bay leaves

Combine ingredients in a bowl and add the meat. Turn in the marinade from time to time. Sufficient for 1–1.5 kg (2–3 lb) of meat.

Lamb or Pork

½ cup olive oil
2 tblspns lemon juice
freshly ground black pepper and rock salt
2 garlic cloves, peeled and cut in half
1 bay leaf
1 sprig of rosemary (optional)

Mix ingredients together in a bowl and add the meat. Cover the bowl. Turn the meat 3 or 4 times during its marination period.

Note: This marinade is also suitable for lamb kebabs. Leg steaks 2.5 cm (1 in) thick cut into cubes are marinated for several hours. Thread the meat on to skewers and grill for 10–12 minutes, turning and basting with the marinade as they cook.

Veal

¼ cup brandy
¼ cup port
2 tblspns olive oil
1 small carrot, sliced
1 small onion, sliced
bouquet garni

Combine ingredients for marinade in a bowl. Add the meat and turn in the marinade from time to time. Sufficient for 1 kg (2 lb) of meat.

TEMPERATURE AND MEASUREMENT EQUIVALENTS

OVEN TEMPERATURES

	Fahrenheit	Celsius
Very slow	250°	120°
Slow	275–300°	140–150°
Moderately slow	325°	160°
Moderate	350°	180°
Moderately hot	375°	190°
Hot	400–450°	200–230°
Very hot	475–500°	250–260°

CUP AND SPOON MEASURES

Measures given in our recipes refer to the standard metric cup and spoon sets approved by the Standards Association of Australia.

A basic metric cup set consists of 1 cup, ½ cup, ⅓ cup and ¼ cup sizes.

The basic spoon set comprises 1 tablespoon, 1 teaspoon, ½ teaspoon and ¼ teaspoon. These sets are available at leading department, kitchen and hardware stores.

FREEZING GUIDE

Store manufactured frozen foods following the instructions on the packages. Most frozen foods should be thawed before cooking and serving.

HOW TO FREEZE

Cakes and desserts	Seal in plastic wrap or foil. Before serving, place on a wire cake rack and thaw out completely.
Fruit and vegetables	Blanch, refresh in cold water, drain thoroughly on absorbent paper and place in airtight containers or freezer bags. Thaw before cooking.
Fish	Clean and scale fish, seal in plastic wrap, foil or freezer bags. Thaw before cooking.
Poultry	Seal completely. Must be thoroughly thawed before cooking.
Meat	Prepare meat for pies and casseroles before freezing. All meat should be placed in airtight containers or freezer bags. Thaw before cooking.

FOOD STORAGE GUIDE

For storage purposes, foods are divided into four categories: non-perishable, perishable, highly perishable and frozen.

• Non-perishable products may last for 12 months or more without deterioration, if stored correctly.

• Perishable foods, when stored correctly, will keep for some time, usually up to 90 days.

• Highly perishable foods should be consumed within two to five days of purchase.

• Frozen products should keep for one to six months depending on the type of food and the temperature maintained in the freezer.

For the best results when freezing or refrigerating foods, follow your refrigerator or freezer manufacturer's guidelines for food storage.

NON-PERISHABLE FOODS

Canned foods	Store in a cool, dry place. Can be refrigerated, although cans might become rusty if left for long periods.
Bottled foods	Store in a cold, dark place.
Cereal products such as flour, spaghetti, salt, sugar, spices, dried beans, and so on	Store in clean, dry, airtight containers.

PERISHABLE FOODS

Bacon	Wrap loosely and store in refrigerator.
Butter and margarine	Refrigerate in sealable containers as these foods absorb other flavours.
Cakes and biscuits	Store separately in clean, airtight containers.
Cheese	Wrap loosely and store in refrigerator.
Coffee	When ground, place in an airtight container and store in the refrigerator.
Eggs	Store carton in refrigerator.
Breakfast cereals	Place in clean, airtight containers or tightly reseal packet.
Tea	Store in an airtight container.
Onions and potatoes	Store in a cool, dark, well-ventilated area.
Root vegetables, pumpkin, pears, apples, oranges	Keep in covered container in the refrigerator or store in a cool, dark place.

HIGHLY PERISHABLE FOODS

Meat and fresh poultry	Loosely cover with greaseproof paper and place in the meat compartment or the coldest part of the refrigerator.
Fresh fish	Place scaled and cleaned fish in an airtight container and refrigerate for one to two days. Fish may be stored for longer periods in the freezer.
Soft fruits (except bananas) and salad vegetables	May be stored in the refrigerator. Melons, strawberries and pineapple should be placed in sealed containers to prevent their flavours penetrating other foods.
Milk and cream	Wipe containers before placing in the refrigerator.
Bread	Leave in plastic wrapper or store in breadbin which must be cleaned and aired frequently. Bread may also be stored in the freezer and slices taken out as needed.

IMPERIAL/METRIC CONVERSION CHART

MASS (WEIGHT)

(Approximate conversions for cookery purposes.)

Imperial	Metric	Imperial	Metric
½ oz	15 g	10 oz	315 g
1 oz	30 g	11 oz	345 g
2 oz	60 g	12 oz (¾ lb)	375 g
3 oz	90 g	13 oz	410 g
4 oz (¼ lb)	125 g	14 oz	440 g
5 oz	155 g	15 oz	470 g
6 oz	185 g	16 oz (1 lb)	500 g (0.5 kg)
7 oz	220 g	24 oz (1½ lb)	750 g
8 oz (½ lb)	250 g	32 oz (2 lb)	1000 g (1 kg)
9 oz	280 g	3 lb	1500 g (1.5 kg)

METRIC CUP AND SPOON SIZES

Cup	Spoon
¼ cup = 60 ml	¼ teaspoon = 1.25 ml
⅓ cup = 80 ml	½ teaspoon = 2.5 ml
½ cup = 125 ml	1 teaspoon = 5 ml
1 cup = 250 ml	1 tablespoon = 20 ml

LIQUIDS

Imperial	Cup*	Metric
1 fl oz		30 ml
2 fl oz	¼ cup	60 ml
3 fl oz		100 ml
4 fl oz	½ cup	125 ml

LIQUIDS (cont'd)

Imperial	Cup*	Metric
5 fl oz (¼ pint)		150 ml
6 fl oz	¾ cup	200 ml
8 fl oz	1 cup	250 ml
10 fl oz (½ pint)	1¼ cups	300 ml
12 fl oz	1½ cups	375 ml
14 fl oz	1¾ cups	425 ml
15 fl oz		475 ml
16 fl oz	2 cups	500 ml
20 fl oz (1 pint)	2½ cups	600 ml

* Cup measures are the same in Imperial and Metric.

LENGTH

Inches	Centimetres	Inches	Centimetres
¼	0.5	7	18
½	1	8	20
¾	2	9	23
1	2.5	10	25
1½	4	12	30
2	5	14	35
2½	6	16	40
3	8	18	45
4	10	20	50
6	15		

NB: 1 cm = 10 mm.

Stir-Fried Pork

500 g (1 lb) minced pork

1 cup water chestnuts, finely chopped

2 tblspns oil

1 clove garlic, crushed

2 tspns curry paste

½ tspn salt

2 tspns soy sauce

pinch of freshly ground pepper

½–¾ cup chicken stock

1 tblspn cornflour

3 tblspns water

1 tblspn chopped fresh coriander

1 Combine pork and water chestnuts, mix well.

2 Heat oil in a heavy-based frying pan, add garlic and curry paste and fry for 2 minutes. Add pork and water chestnuts and fry for 1 minute. Add salt, soy sauce and pepper and cook for 2–3 minutes or until pork is browned.

3 Add stock and bring to boil. Cook without lid for 3–4 minutes.

4 Mix cornflour with water and stir into mixture. Bring to the boil again, reduce heat and cook until thickened.

5 Stir in coriander and serve.

Serves 4

Pork and Potato Stew

750 g (1½ lb) stewing pork, diced

2 tblspns oil

2 cloves garlic, crushed

3 tspns grated fresh root ginger

2 tspns chilli powder

1 tspn turmeric

425 g (14 oz) can tomato puree

¾ cup chicken stock

2 cups frozen or fresh peas

1 tspn ground cumin

500 g (1 lb) new potatoes, peeled

salt and pepper

1 Remove fat or sinew from pork. Heat oil in a large, heavy-based frying pan, add garlic, ginger, chilli powder and turmeric, and fry over moderate heat for 2 minutes.

2 Add pork pieces and fry over high heat, tossing all the time until pork is golden, about 5 minutes.

3 Add tomato puree, chicken stock, peas and cumin, and mix well. Bring to the boil.

4 Cover pan with a lid, lower heat and simmer for 1 hour, or until pork is almost tender.

5 Add potatoes and season to taste with salt and pepper. Simmer without a lid for a further 20 minutes, or until potatoes are cooked.

Serves 6

Peanut Spiced Pork

750 g (1½ lb) pork neck

1 tblspn oil for frying

MARINADE

½ cup crunchy peanut butter

2 tspns soy sauce

2 tspns brown sugar

2 fresh red chillies, seeded and diced

2 tspns lemon juice

2 tblspns white vinegar

1 tblspn oil

1 tblspn water

1 Slice pork thinly. Heat oil in a large, heavy-based frying pan, add pork slices and fry over moderate heat for 1–2 minutes or until pork changes colour.

2 Mix all marinade ingredients together until well combined, then pour over pork. Marinate pork for at least 2 hours.

3 Place pork in a single layer in a large baking dish, pour over marinade and bake in a moderate oven (180°C) for 30–40 minutes or until pork is tender and brown.

Serves 4

THE EXOTIC SIDE OF LAMB

Few meats lend themselves better to spicy methods of cooking than lamb. These traditional favourites are sure to please.

Spicy Lamb and Vegetables

1.5 kg (3 lb) boneless lamb (use leg or shoulder)

45 g (1½ oz) butter or margarine

2 onions, thinly sliced

1 cup beef stock

juice of 3 lemons

1 tspn ground cumin

1 tspn ground coriander

salt and freshly ground pepper

1 medium eggplant (aubergine), chopped

500 g (1 lb) new potatoes

300 g (10 oz) fresh or frozen peas

1 tblspn cornflour

¼ cup cold water

1 Cut meat into large chunks. Melt butter or margarine in a large saucepan, add lamb and fry over high heat until browned on all sides. Remove from pan.

2 Add onions to pan, lower heat and cook until onion has softened.

3 Return meat to pan, add beef stock, lemon juice, cumin and coriander. Season to taste with salt and pepper. Bring to the boil. Cover with a lid and simmer gently for 1 hour.

4 Add eggplant (aubergine), potatoes and peas and simmer for a further 45 minutes or until lamb and vegetables are tender.

5 Mix cornflour with cold water to form a smooth paste. Pour into casserole and mix well. Bring to the boil, stirring all the time until sauce has thickened, about 5 minutes.

Serves 6

Lamb with Curried Banana Stuffing

1.5 kg (3 lb) boned loin or leg of lamb

salt and pepper

1 tblspn lemon juice

200 ml (¾ cup) natural yoghurt

1 tblspn curry paste

2 tblspns crunchy peanut butter

¼ cup chopped fresh coriander

4 green bananas

¼ cup peanuts

1 tblspn flour

1 cup chicken stock

1 Place loin or leg of lamb on a board, fat side down. Season surface with salt and pepper and sprinkle with lemon juice.

2 Mix together yoghurt, curry paste, peanut butter and coriander and spread three-quarters of this mixture over the surface of the meat. (The remainder is for sauce.)

Spicy Lamb and Vegetables

3 Peel bananas and cut in halves lengthwise. Arrange in rows over yoghurt mixture, sprinkle with peanuts.

4 Roll up loin or leg and tie securely with string. Place meat in baking dish and bake in a moderate oven (180ºC) for 1–1½ hours or until tender. Remove meat from pan and keep warm.

5 Place baking dish on top of stove, add flour and cook over moderate heat, stirring until golden brown, about 2 minutes.

6 Stir in chicken stock and cook, stirring, until sauce boils and thickens, about 2 minutes. Add reserved yoghurt mixture, cook for a further 1 minute or until sauce is heated through.

7 Slice lamb and serve with sauce.

Serves 8

Curried Lamb Chops

10-12 lamb chump or loin chops

seasoned flour

2 tblspns oil

2 onions, chopped

1 clove garlic, crushed

1½ tspns curry powder

1½ cups chicken stock

2 tomatoes, peeled and chopped

1 tblspn brown sugar

3 tblspns vinegar

3 tblspns tomato paste

6 tspns soy sauce

1 Trim excess fat from chops. Coat chops with seasoned flour, shaking off any excess.

2 Heat oil in a large, heavy-based frying pan, add chops and fry a few at a time over high heat, until golden brown, about 5 minutes each side. Remove chops from pan and drain on absorbent paper. Place chops in a deep, ovenproof casserole dish.

3 Pour off all but 2 tablespoonsful of fat from pan. Add onions, garlic and curry powder, and fry over moderate heat until onion softens slightly, about 3 minutes.

4 Add all remaining ingredients to the pan and bring to the boil. Lower heat and simmer until liquid has reduced slightly, about 7–8 minutes.

5 Pour mixture over chops. Cook without lid in a moderate oven (180°C) for 1 hour, or until chops are tender. Turn chops a few times during cooking. Spoon or skim off any fat from the sauce before serving. Serve with noodles or rice.

Serves 6

Fruity Lamb Curry

1.5 kg (3 lb) boneless lamb, cut into 2.5 cm (1 in) cubes

¼ cup plain flour

2 tspns curry powder

2 tblspns oil

3 onions, chopped

3 stalks celery, diced

3 carrots, peeled and sliced

2 apples, peeled and sliced

1 cup canned apricot nectar

1 cup chicken stock

salt and pepper

2 tblspns chopped mint

2 tblspns chopped parsley

150 ml (¼ pint) natural yoghurt

1 Toss lamb cubes lightly in a mixture of flour and curry powder, shaking off any excess. Heat oil in a large, heavy-based saucepan or frying pan, add lamb and fry over high heat until golden, about 8–10 minutes. You will need to do this in several batches. Set lamb aside.

2 Add onion, celery and carrot to pan and cook over moderate heat until onion has softened slightly, about 4 minutes.

Curried Lamb Chops

3 Add apples, apricot nectar, stock and lamb, season to taste with salt and pepper, stir until well mixed. Bring to the boil, lower heat and simmer without a lid for 1½ hours or until lamb is tender.

4 Add mint, parsley and yoghurt, mix well and cook until heated through, about 3 minutes. Serve hot with rice.

Serves 8

Skewered Lamb with Sate Sauce

MARINADE

¾ cup Coconut Milk (see page 36)

440g (14oz) can pineapple pieces, drained and juice reserved

¼ cup soy sauce

pinch of chilli powder

few drops chilli sauce

2 cloves garlic, crushed

2 tblspns tomato paste

SKEWERS

1kg (2lb) lean lamb, cut into cubes

2 large onions, cut into wedges

1 green capsicum (green pepper), seeded and cut into chunks

½ cup crunchy peanut butter

1 Mix together Coconut Milk, pineapple juice, soy sauce, chilli powder, chilli sauce, garlic and tomato paste. Marinate lamb and onions in this mixture for at least 4 hours. Drain, reserving marinade.

2 Thread alternate pieces of lamb, onion, green capsicum and pineapple pieces onto skewers. Cook under a hot grill until cooked, about 10–15 minutes, brushing with a little of the marinade during the cooking.

3 Add peanut butter to remaining marinade and boil until sauce thickens. Check for flavour, adding more chilli sauce if you like it hot.

4 Serve lamb skewers on a bed of rice with a little sauce poured over the top. Serve remaining sauce separately.

Serves 6

Lamb Kofta

SAUSAGES

750g (1½ lb) mince or ground lamb

2 onions, finely chopped

1 clove garlic, crushed

½ cup chopped parsley

½ cup chopped fresh mint

1 tblspn paprika

1½ tspns curry powder

1 egg, lightly beaten

salt and pepper to taste

oil for grilling

YOGHURT SAUCE

1 cup natural yoghurt

1 tblspn chopped fresh coriander

salt and pepper

¼ tspn ground ginger

1 Place all sausage ingredients in large mixing bowl. Using your hands, mix until ingredients are well combined.

2 Form mixture into small oval sausages about 7cm (3in) long and 2cm (1in) thick.

3 Push onto bamboo skewers and press firmly, moulding into shape with your fingers. Place skewers on plate and cover with plastic wrap. Chill for 1 hour.

4 Mix all sauce ingredients together until well combined. Cover with plastic wrap and refrigerate until ready to serve.

5 Preheat grill to high. Brush grill tray well with oil to prevent sticking and place skewers under grill. Cook until brown and firm to touch, about 10 minutes, turning a few times during cooking. Slip sausages off skewers and serve with Yoghurt Sauce.

Serves 6

Lamb Kofta

HOT FAVOURITES WITH VEGETABLES

Eastern cultures have embraced vegetarian dishes for centuries. That's how they've perfected such nutritious and flavoursome meals.

Curried Beans

1 cup mixed dried beans

1 tblspn ghee or oil

1 onion, finely chopped

1 clove garlic, crushed

1 red capsicum (red pepper), seeded and sliced

2 tspns curry paste

2 tomatoes, roughly chopped

½ cup chicken stock

½ tspn salt

1 tblspn lemon juice

salt and pepper

1 Wash and soak beans in cold water overnight. Drain and place in large saucepan with 8 cups water. Bring to boil and boil 45 minutes to 1 hour or until beans are tender. Drain and reserve liquid.

2 Heat ghee or oil in large frying pan or saucepan. Add onion, garlic and capsicum and fry for 6 minutes.

3 Add curry paste and tomatoes, mix well and cook for 5 minutes.

4 Add beans, stock and salt and cook for 5 minutes. Stir in lemon juice and season to taste with salt and pepper.

Serves 4–6

Chilli Green Beans

2 tblspns oil

2 onions, thickly sliced

1 tspn chilli powder

1 tblspn flour

1 cup chicken stock

500 g (1 lb) green beans

1 capsicum or red pepper, seeded and sliced

1 tspn tomato paste

salt and pepper

4 tomatoes, peeled and quartered

1 Heat oil in a heavy-based saucepan. Add onion and fry until onion has softened, about 6–8 minutes.

2 Add chilli powder and flour and cook, stirring, for 2 minutes.

3 Gradually add stock, stirring until sauce is smooth.

4 Add beans, capsicum and tomato paste and bring to the boil. Lower heat and simmer for 15 minutes. Season to taste with salt and pepper.

5 Add tomatoes and cook for a further 3 minutes.

Serves 4

Curried Beans

Curried Tomatoes

4-5 large tomatoes

2 tblspns oil

3 spring onions (scallions), sliced

1 clove garlic, crushed

2 tspns curry paste

½ bunch spinach (approximately 5 leaves), washed and finely shredded

100 g (3½ oz) cooked peas, mashed

1 Wash tomatoes, pat dry with absorbent paper. Cut a slice from tops of tomatoes and reserve. Scoop out seeds and flesh from tomatoes and set aside.

2 Heat oil in a large, heavy-based saucepan, add onion and garlic and fry until onion has softened slightly, about 5 minutes.

3 Add curry paste and fry, stirring constantly for 2 minutes.

4 Stir in spinach, tomato pulp and peas and mix to combine. Cook, stirring occasionally, for 5 minutes or until spinach has wilted.

5 Fill mixture into tomato shells and replace tops. Place on a baking tray and cover with foil. Cook in a moderately hot oven (190ºC) for 10–15 minutes, or until tomatoes are cooked.

Serves 4

Curried Tomatoes

Cauliflower and Nut Curry

1 tblspn oil

1 onion, finely chopped

2 tspns curry powder

½ cup chopped cashews

½ cup cream

1 cauliflower, broken into florets

250 g (8 oz) peas

1 Heat oil in a small saucepan. Add onion and curry powder and fry, stirring occasionally, for 8 minutes or until onion has softened. Stir in cashews and cook for a further 10 minutes. Add cream, mix well and bring to the boil. Lower heat and simmer 5 minutes.

2 Meanwhile cook cauliflower and peas in a saucepan of boiling salted water for 10 minutes or until cooked but still firm. Drain and return to the saucepan. Pour over curry cream sauce, mix lightly and cook until heated through.

Serves 6–8

Curried Lentils

2 tblspns butter, margarine or ghee

½ cup chopped spring onions (scallions)

4 carrots, thinly sliced

4 stalks celery, cut into 2 cm (1 in) lengths

1½ tspns curry powder

1 tblspn wholemeal flour

4 cups vegetable or chicken stock

½ cup peanut butter

½ small cauliflower, broken into florets

¾ cup split red lentils

½ bunch spinach (approximately 5 leaves), washed and finely shredded

¼ cup natural yoghurt

salt and pepper

1 Heat butter, margarine or ghee in a heavy-based saucepan, add spring onions (scallions), carrot and celery and fry, stirring occasionally, until vegetables have softened, about 10 minutes.

2 Remove pan from heat, stir in curry powder and flour, mixing well. Return pan to heat, cook for 1 minute then gradually add stock. Cook, stirring until sauce boils and thickens, about 3 minutes.

3 Add peanut butter, cauliflower and lentils, lower heat and simmer covered with a lid for 20 minutes or until lentils are tender.

4 Stir through spinach, simmer without a lid for 5 minutes or until spinach has wilted slightly.

5 Add yoghurt and season to taste with salt and pepper. Continue cooking until heated through, about 2 minutes.

Serves 6

Vegetable Fritters

1 cup self-raising flour

salt and freshly ground black pepper

1 tspn curry powder

1 egg

½ cup water

2 tblspns milk

2 cups cooked, chopped vegetables

oil for frying

1 Sift flour, salt, pepper and curry powder into a mixing bowl. Make a well in the centre, add egg, then gradually stir in the water and milk.

2 Beat mixture until the batter is smooth. Add the cooked vegetables and stir until well coated with the batter.

3 Heat oil in a deep, heavy-based saucepan or deep fryer. When hot, drop tablespoonsful of the mixture into the oil and cook until puffed and golden brown, about 3 minutes. Drain on absorbent paper and serve hot.

Makes 24

Potato and Spinach Curry

1 tblspn ghee or oil

1 onion, thinly sliced

1 tspn grated fresh root ginger

1 tspn turmeric

½ tspn chilli powder

½ tspn salt

750 g (1½ lb) new potatoes, scrubbed

½ bunch spinach (approximately 5 leaves)

1 tspn garam masala

¼ cup toasted almonds, roughly chopped

1 Heat ghee in a large, heavy-based saucepan. Add onion and ginger and fry for 8 minutes or until onion has softened. Add spices and salt and fry, stirring constantly, for 2 minutes.

2 Add potatoes to saucepan with 3 tablespoons water and cover saucepan with a lid. Bring to the boil, then lower heat and simmer for 10 minutes or until potatoes are almost tender.

3 Wash spinach and shred (with stalks). Add to saucepan, cover with a lid and cook for 15–20 minutes or until vegetables are tender.

4 Stir in garam masala and almonds. Cook for 2 minutes to heat through.

Serves 6

Yoghurt Topped Potatoes

500 g (1 lb) small potatoes, scrubbed

½ cup natural yoghurt

¼ cup cream

½ tspn ground coriander

¼ tspn chilli powder

½ tspn turmeric

½ tspn garam masala

1 Cook whole potatoes in a saucepan of boiling salted water for 10–15 minutes or until amost tender but still firm. Drain and cool slightly. Cut potatoes into thin slices and place in a lightly greased baking dish.

2 Mix yoghurt, cream and spices together, pour over potatoes and cook in a moderately slow oven (160ºC) for 15–20 minutes or until yoghurt topping is firm and golden.

Serves 4

Curried Fruit and Vegetables

250 g (½ lb) green beans

500 g (1 lb) fresh broad beans

½ small cauliflower

250 g (½ lb) apricots

1 tblspn curry powder

1 tblspn flour

2 onions, thinly sliced

2 tblspns oil

1⅔ cups stock

2 tblspns chutney

salt and pepper

2 tomatoes, peeled and quartered

1 Cut the beans into 3 pieces, and pod the broad beans. Break cauliflower into large florets and halve and stone the apricots. Mix the curry powder and flour together.

2 Toss all the vegetables and fruit in the curry powder and flour mixture. Heat oil in a large, heavy-based frying pan, add vegetables and fruit and fry, stirring constantly for 3 minutes.

3 Add the stock and chutney, season with salt and pepper. Cover the pan with a lid and simmer for 15 minutes. Add tomatoes to the pan and cook for 2 minutes. Serve hot with rice.

Serves 6

Clockwise from top left: Potato and Spinach Curry, Pineapple and Cucumber Sambal (page 64), Curried Fruit and Vegetables and Vegetable Fritters (page 51).

Mixed Vegetable Curry

1 tblspn ghee or oil

3 onions, sliced

2 cloves garlic, crushed

1 tblspn garam masala

2 tspns curry paste

250 g (8 oz) button mushrooms

500 g (1 lb) potatoes, peeled and cubed

2 carrots, thickly sliced

2 stalks celery, sliced

1 cup fresh or frozen peas

½ cup vegetable stock

salt and pepper

1 Heat ghee or oil in a large, heavy-based saucepan, add onions and garlic and fry over moderate heat for 3 minutes, or until onion has softened slight.

2 Add garam masala and curry paste and fry, stirring all the time for 1 minute.

3 Add mushrooms, potatoes, carrots, celery, peas and stock and bring to the boil. Season to taste with salt and pepper.

4 Lower heat, cover pan with a lid and simmer for 30 minutes, or until vegetables are tender. Stir occasionally during cooking.

Serves 4

Eggplant and Potato Curry

3 medium eggplants (aubergines), stalks removed

4 large potatoes, peeled

salt

½ cup oil

3 onions, quartered, separated into petals

1 bunch snake beans or 8 oz green beans

2 cloves garlic, crushed

2 tspns grated fresh root ginger

½ tspn cumin seeds, ground

½ tspn turmeric

1 or 2 green chillies, seeded and diced

1 tspn salt

1 tspn brown sugar

3 tblspns tomato paste

1¼ cups water

1 Cut eggplants (aubergines) and potatoes into large cubes. Sprinkle eggplant with salt and set aside for 30 minutes. Drain off liquid, rinse and dry eggplant.

2 Heat 2 tablespoons of the oil in a large, heavy-based saucepan, add eggplant cubes and fry for 3 minutes. Remove from pan.

3 Add another 2 tablespoonsful of oil to pan and fry potatoes, tossing and turning until golden brown, about 5 minutes. Remove from pan and set aside.

4 Add remaining oil to saucepan and fry onions and beans for 3 minutes or until onions have softened slightly.

5 Stir in garlic, ginger, cumin, turmeric and chilli and cook for a further 1 minute.

6 Add salt, brown sugar, tomato paste, water, eggplants and potatoes. Bring to the boil, lower the heat and simmer, covered with a lid, until vegetables are tender, about 20 minutes. Stir occasionally during cooking.

Serves 10

Mixed Vegetable Curry

RICE AND NOODLES

In many parts of the world, rice and noodles form a staple part of every meal. They're not only nutritious, they also temper spicy food.

Bamie Goreng

250 g (½ lb) thin egg noodles

3 tblspns oil

1 clove garlic, crushed

1 cm (½ in) piece fresh root ginger, finely chopped

2 chicken fillets, cut into strips

250 g (½ lb) green prawns if available, or tinned shrimps, peeled and chopped

4 white cabbage leaves, shredded

1 stalk celery, sliced

3 carrots, peeled and sliced

salt and pepper

1 cup chicken stock

1 tblspn soy sauce

red chillies

1 Cook noodles in a saucepan of boiling salted water for 3 minutes. Drain, rinse under cold running water and drain again.

2 Heat oil in a large frying pan, add garlic and ginger and fry for 1 minute.

3 Add chicken and prawns and fry, stirring for 3 minutes or until chicken is white and prawns pink.

4 Add vegetables and cook, stirring constantly for a further 3 minutes.

5 Stir in noodles, salt and pepper to taste and stock and bring to the boil. Stir in soy sauce.

6 Pile onto a warm serving platter and garnish with chopped red chillies.

Serves 4

Nasi Goreng

2 cups long-grain rice

3½ cups water

1 tspn salt

125 g (4 oz) unsalted butter or ghee

2 large onions, chopped

2 tspns curry powder

250 g (8 oz) lean pork, cut into thin strips

2 tspns soy sauce

salt and pepper

3 cups cooked vegetables

GARNISH

1 egg

1 tblspn water

salt and pepper

15 g (½ oz) butter or margarine

tomatoes

spring onions (scallions)

lettuce

cucumber

Bamie Goreng (right) and Nasi Goreng (top)

1 Place rice, water and salt in a heavy-based saucepan and bring to a full rolling boil over high heat, then turn heat as low as it will go, cover pan tightly and cook for 20 minutes. Remove from heat and let steam escape for a few minutes before forking rice onto a shallow tray. Allow to cool and store in the refrigerator until ready to use.

2 Melt 60 g (2 oz) butter or ghee in a large frying pan. Add onions and cook until lightly browned. Add curry powder and cook for 2 minutes, then add pork and cook until well browned and tender, about 15 minutes.

3 Add remaining butter or ghee, soy sauce and half the rice. Season well with salt and pepper. Continue to cook until the rice is heated, stirring and tossing.

4 Add vegetables and remaining rice. Mix well and when heated thoroughly, turn out onto a large flat heated plate.

5 Break egg into a small bowl, add water, salt and pepper and beat well with a fork.

6 Melt 15 g (½ oz) butter in a small frying pan. Add egg mixture and cook over moderate heat until egg is set and brown underneath. Turn omelette over to brown the other side. Remove from the pan, cool and cut into thin strips.

7 Garnish rice dish with thin strips of omelette and place wedges of tomato and spring onions around the outside. Serve immediately with a salad of lettuce and cucumber.

Serves 6

Pilau Rice

60 g (2 oz) ghee or oil

1 onion, finely chopped

½ tspn ground turmeric

8 whole peppercorns

2 whole cloves

4 cardamom seeds

7.5 cm (3 in) cinnamon stick

2 cups long-grain rice

3½ cups chicken stock

salt and pepper to taste

½ cup sultanas

1 cup frozen peas

toasted almonds for garnish

1 Heat ghee in a large saucepan, add half the onion and fry until onion has softened slightly, about 4 minutes. Add spices and fry, stirring constantly for 2–3 minutes. Add rice and cook, stirring for 2 minutes.

2 Add stock and salt and pepper to taste. Bring to the boil, add remaining onion. Cover saucepan with a lid and cook over low heat for 20 minutes or until nearly all the liquid has been absorbed.

3 Lightly stir in sultanas and peas and cook, covered with a lid, for a further 5 minutes. Remove lid to allow steam to escape then spoon onto a serving dish. Scatter almonds on top and serve.

Serves 6–8

Egg Noodles with Hot Sauce

250 g (8 oz) fine egg noodles

1 tblspn oil

2 cloves garlic, finely chopped

1 tspn finely chopped fresh root ginger

250 g (8 oz) pork mince

250 g (8 oz) green prawns, finely chopped (if available) or tinned shrimps

2 red chillies, seeded and diced

1 red capsicum, seeded and cut into thin strips

4 spring onions (scallions), finely chopped

½ tspn sugar

1 tblspn soy sauce

1 tblspn dry sherry

1 cup water

3 tspns cornflour

Egg Noodles with Hot Sauce

1 Soak the egg noodles in hot water for 10 minutes, drain. Cook noodles in a pan of boiling salted water for 3–4 minutes. Drain and run cold water over them. Stand in a colander over a pan of boiling water to keep warm.

2 Heat oil in a heavy-based frying pan. Add garlic and ginger and cook, stirring for 1 minute. Add the pork mince and fry, pressing down with a fork until meat is brown and crumbly, about 2 minutes.

3 Add prawns, chillies, capsicum, spring onions (scallions), sugar, soy sauce, sherry and water. Mix well then bring to the boil. Mix cornflour with a little water to a smooth paste.

4 Stir cornflour mixture into the boiling sauce. Bring to the boil, lower the heat and cook, stirring until the sauce has thickened, about 3–4 minutes.

5 Place noodles on a serving plate and pour over the sauce.

Serves 4

Coconut Rice

2½ cups milk

1 cup desiccated coconut

⅓ cup oil

3 cups long-grain rice

2 large onions, finely chopped

1 clove garlic, crushed

½ tspn turmeric

¼ tspn ground cinnamon

2½ cups water

⅔ cup toasted almonds

⅔ cup sultanas

¾ cup cooked peas

salt and pepper

1 Heat milk and coconut in a heavy-based saucepan until milk comes to the boil, reduce heat and simmer without a lid for 3 minutes. Set aside.

2 Heat oil in a heavy-based saucepan, add rice, onions, garlic, turmeric and cinnamon and fry for 3 minutes, stirring constantly. Add milk mixture and water, cover with a lid and simmer very gently for 30 minutes or until all liquid is absorbed and rice is tender. Do not stir as rice may become mushy.

3 If mixture becomes too dry before rice is cooked add a little extra water and continue cooking until rice is tender. Just before serving toss through almonds, sultanas and peas and season to taste with salt and pepper. Heat gently and serve.

Serves 8–10

Lamb Yoghurt Pilaf

750 g (1½ lb) boneless lamb, cubed

juice of 2 lemons

¾ cup cream

½ cup natural yoghurt

1½ cups beef stock

4 whole cloves

1 tblspn butter, margarine or ghee

1 onion, finely chopped

1 tblspn poppy seeds

¼ tspn ground cardamom

½ cinnamon stick

2 bay leaves

4 spinach leaves, washed and shredded

1½ cups raw rice

extra ghee or butter

1 red pepper, seeded and sliced

1 onion, sliced

1 Place lamb cubes in a large bowl. Add lemon juice, cream and yoghurt and stir until lamb is well coated with the cream mixture. Cover bowl with plastic wrap and refrigerate for at least 2 hours to allow the flavour to develop.

2 Place stock and cloves in a small saucepan and bring to the boil. Cover pan with a lid, lower heat and simmer for 5 minutes. Remove pan from heat and strain the liquid. Set liquid aside.

3 Melt butter, margarine or ghee in a deep, heavy-based saucepan. Add onion, poppy seeds and cardamom. Fry over moderate heat, stirring occasionally until onion has softened slightly, about 3 minutes.

4 Place cinnamon stick and bay leaves on a small square of muslin and tie up. Add to fried onion with meat, cream marinade, half a cup of the clove-flavoured stock and spinach. Mix well and bring to the boil. Cover pan with a lid, lower the heat and simmer gently for 1½ hours or until meat is tender.

5 Stir in the rice and remaining clove-flavoured stock and bring to the boil. Cover pan with a lid, lower the heat and simmer for 20 minutes or until rice is tender and most of the liquid has been absorbed. Remove muslin bag before serving.

6 Garnish with pepper mixture. Fifteen minutes before Pilaf is finished, melt ghee or butter in a heavy-based frying pan. Add pepper and onion and cook until golden, about 8–10 minutes.

Serves 6–8

Lamb Yoghurt Pilaf

BREADS AND SAMBALS

Many of the basic dishes in this book become a banquet when you serve them with an array of breads and sambals. Some will cool you down, others add extra spice.

Curry Yoghurt Sauce

1 cup natural yoghurt

¼ cup sour cream

1 tblspn apricot jam

1 tblspn peach chutney

2 tspns tomato sauce

1 tspn curry powder

1 tspn turmeric

salt and pepper

1 Mix ingredients together in a bowl. Season to taste.

Makes 1¼ cups

Chilli Nut Sauce

2 tspns coriander seeds, ground

1 tspn cumin seeds, ground

1 clove garlic, crushed

8 spring onions (scallions), chopped

3 dried chillies, soaked

100 g (4 oz) cashew nuts

1 tblspn oil

155 g (5 oz) roasted peanuts, ground

1 cup thick Coconut Milk (see page 36)

¼ tspn salt

Clockwise from top: Chilli Sauce, Curry Yoghurt Sauce, Apricot Chutney, Lemon Chutney and Chilli Nut Sauce.

1 Place coriander, cumin, garlic, spring onions (scallions), chillies and cashews in a food processor or electric blender and process to a fine paste.

2 Heat oil in a frying pan, add spice and nut paste and fry, stirring constantly, for 3 minutes. Add peanuts and cook for 1 minute. Stir in Coconut Milk and salt, and bring to the boil.

3 Lower heat and simmer for 5–7 minutes or until sauce thickens. If necessary add lemon juice or sugar to taste.

Makes approximately 1½ cups

Lemon Chutney

4 large lemons

2 medium onions

1 tblspn salt

2 cups malt vinegar

2 cups sugar

¾ cup raisins

1 tblspn mustard seeds

1 tspn ground ginger

pinch cayenne pepper

1 Wash and slice lemons and discard pips. Peel and slice onions and place in glass bowl with sliced lemons. Sprinkle with salt and leave for 24 hours.

2 Drain off excess liquid.

3 Place lemons and onions in a large saucepan. Add the remaining ingredients, bring to boil and simmer gently until lemons are tender, about 45 minutes.

4 Spoon into hot sterilised jars and seal.

Makes 4 jars

Apricot Chutney

1 large apple, peeled, cored and chopped

1 kg (2 lb) apricots, chopped

1 large onion, chopped

2 tspns mixed pickling spices (in a muslin bag)

1¼ cups malt vinegar

½ cup sultanas

½ tspn salt

310 g (10 oz) sugar

1 Place fruit and onion in a large preserving pan or saucepan with the spices and half the vinegar. Bring to the boil, then lower heat and simmer until fruit softens.

2 Gradually stir in remaining vinegar, sultanas, salt and sugar. Cook, stirring until sugar has dissolved, then cook until chutney is the consistency of jam.

3 Fill warm sterilised jars with chutney to within 5 mm (¼ in) of the top. If using metal covers, protect chutney with a layer of wax and a round of cardboard before sealing. Store in a cool, dry place.

Makes 3 jars

Pineapple and Cucumber Sambal

1 cup canned pineapple pieces, drained

½ cucumber, sliced

1 tspn shredded or desiccated coconut

Mix together the pineapple and cucumber slices. Chill in the refrigerator for a few hours then serve sprinkled with coconut.

Serves 6–8

Banana and Date in Yoghurt

2 bananas, sliced

2 tspns lemon juice

1 cup dates, pitted and chopped

1 cup natural yoghurt

mint leaves for decoration

Dip banana slices in lemon juice to prevent them discolouring. Mix bananas with remaining ingredients. Spoon into a serving bowl and garnish with mint leaves.

Serves 6–8

Tomato and Mint Sambal

4 ripe, firm tomatoes, chopped, or 1 punnet cherry tomatoes, halved

¼ cup chopped mint

¼ cup oil

salt and pepper

Combine all ingredients, spoon into serving bowls and chill.

Serves 6–8

Onion Rings

Peel and cut 2 onions into very thin rings. Soak in cold water for 1 hour, drain, and serve dusted with chopped mint.

Clockwise from centre left: Banana and Date in Yoghurt, Tomato and Mint Sambal, Pineapple and Cucumber Sambal, Peanut Sambal and Melon Sambal.

Melon Salad

1 rockmelon (cantaloupe) and 1 honeydew melon (2 of 1 type may be used)

500g (1 lb) tomatoes

1 large cucumber

2 tblspns vinegar

salt and freshly ground pepper

1 tblspn chopped parsley

1 tspn each chopped mint and chives

1 Cut melons in quarters, remove seeds and skin. Cut into cubes. Peel and quarter tomatoes, squeeze out seeds, remove core and cut each quarter in half if tomatoes are large. Peel cucumber, halve lengthwise, remove seeds and cut across into chunks.

2 Mix all together in a deep bowl. Whisk vinegar with seasonings and add herbs. Pour over salad, cover and chill for 2 hours before serving.

Serves 6

Peanut Sambal

⅓ cup peanut oil

½ tspn prawn paste (optional)

1 onion, finely chopped

2 cloves garlic, crushed

1 or 2 hot chillies, seeded and diced

1 cup roasted peanuts, finely chopped

2 small tomatoes, chopped

3 tblspns brown sugar

salt to taste

⅓ cup water

1 Heat oil in a heavy-based frying pan, add prawn paste, onion, garlic and chillies. Fry for 4 minutes without letting the mixture burn.

2 Stir in peanuts, tomatoes, sugar, salt and water. Continue cooking over low heat, stirring frequently, until oil rises to the top of the mixture, about 4–5 minutes.

3 Remove from heat and set aside until ready to serve. Serve cold.

Serves 6

Cucumbers in Yoghurt

1 cucumber

1 tspn salt

¼ tspn freshly grated root ginger

1 clove garlic, crushed

½ cup natural yoghurt

chopped mint or parsley

1 Peel cucumber and slice thinly. Sprinkle with salt and allow to stand for 30 minutes. Drain off the liquid.

2 Add ginger, garlic and yoghurt. Mix well, adding more salt if necessary. Chill. Serve sprinkled with chopped mint or parsley.

Serves 4–6

Pineapple Chutney

500g (1 lb) peeled and chopped pineapple

2 tspns salt

5 cloves garlic, crushed

5cm (2 in) piece fresh root ginger, peeled and cut into small pieces

1 onion, peeled and quartered

¾ cup sultanas

1 cup raw sugar

2 cups white vinegar

1 tspn allspice

½ tspn nutmeg

1 Place chopped pineapple in a colander, sprinkle salt over pineapple and allow to stand for 2 hours. Wash under cold running water and drain well.

2 Place garlic, ginger, onion and sultanas in an electric blender or food processor, and process for 1 minute, or until ingredients are minced and well combined.

Dahl.

3 Place sugar and vinegar in a medium-size, heavy-based saucepan and cook over low heat, stirring all the time, until sugar has dissolved.

4 Add pineapple, sultana mixture and spices to vinegar, and bring to the boil. Simmer for 45 minutes, or until pineapple is soft and nearly all liquid has evaporated. Stir occasionally during cooking.

5 Allow to cool, pour into clean sterilised jars. Seal tightly, and store in the refrigerator.

Note: This chutney will keep for at least 4 months.

Makes 2 cups

Onion and Tomato Salad

2 onions, roughly chopped

1 tblspn salt

3 ripe, firm tomatoes, roughly chopped

1 green chilli, seeded and finely chopped

2 spring onions (scallions), sliced

1 clove garlic, crushed

1 tspn finely chopped fresh root ginger

1 tblspn brown sugar

1 tblspn white vinegar

1 Place onion slices on a plate, sprinkle with salt and set aside for 1 hour. Squeeze well to remove any liquid from onions, rinse then drain on absorbent paper.

2 Place onions and remaining ingredients except brown sugar and white vinegar in a bowl. Mix together the sugar and vinegar, pour over salad mixture and toss gently. Spoon into a serving dish.

Serves 6–8

Dahl

4 tblspns ghee

2 onions, finely chopped

375 g (12 oz) dried red lentils, washed and drained

1 tspn ground cumin

3 tspns curry paste

4½ cups water

2 tomatoes, chopped

salt and pepper

extra chopped tomato for garnish

1 Heat ghee in a medium-size, heavy-based saucepan, add onions and fry over moderate heat until golden, about 10 minutes.

2 Add drained lentils, cumin and curry paste, and cook for 1–2 minutes. Add water and simmer without a lid until liquid is almost absorbed, about 20 minutes.

3 Stir in tomatoes and season to taste with salt and pepper. Continue cooking for a further 5 minutes. Garnish with extra chopped tomato and serve.

Serves 6

Mixed Pickles

250 g (8 oz) carrots

250 g (8 oz) green beans

500 g (1 lb) pickling onions

500 g (1 lb) cauliflower

2 cucumbers

4 fresh chillies

250 g (8 oz) salt

2.4 litres (5 pints) water

SPICED VINEGAR

1.2 litres (2½ pints) white vinegar

1 tblspn celery and mustard seeds

5 cm (2 in) cinnamon stick

1 tspn peppercorns

5 cm (2 in) piece fresh root ginger

1 tspn allspice berries

1 cup sugar

1 Scrape carrots and string beans. Cut into 1.5 cm (½ in) slices. Peel onions. Break cauliflower into florets.

2 Cut cucumbers into quarters then into 2.5 cm (1 in) pieces. Leave chillies whole. Mix salt and water in a large bowl and add prepared vegetables. Let stand overnight.

3 Combine ingredients for Spiced Vinegar, cook over gentle heat, stirring all the time until sugar has dissolved, then bring to boil. Add drained vegetables and simmer until heated through.

4 Pack vegetables into hot sterilised jars. Bring liquid to boil and fill jars. Seal and label. These are best made several weeks before using.

Makes 6 jars

Curried Scones

2 cups self-raising flour

1 tspn curry powder

1 tspn salt

1 tblspn finely chopped onion

1 tblspn finely chopped parsley

2 tblspns grated cheese

1 cup milk

1 tblspn melted butter or margarine

extra milk

1 Set oven temperature at hot (220ºC). Sift flour, curry powder and salt into a large bowl. Add onion, parsley and grated cheese.

2 Make a well in the centre of the mixture and quickly pour in the milk and the melted butter. Stir until combined.

3 Turn out onto a lightly floured board and knead lightly. Cut into rounds. Place on a lightly greased baking tray. Brush with milk and bake in a preheated oven for 15 minutes. Serve hot.

Makes 16

Chapatis

2 cups wholemeal flour

½–¾ cup warm water

1 Sift flour into a bowl, add water and mix to a soft but not sticky dough. Knead dough on a lightly floured work surface for 10 minutes or until dough is smooth.

2 Cover dough with a damp cloth and leave to rest for 1 hour.

3 Knead lightly on a floured surface. Divide dough into 8 pieces and roll each piece into a ball. Flatten each ball slightly with hands and roll out to a 15 cm (6 in) circle.

4 Heat a heavy-based frying pan. Place one chapati at a time in frying pan and cook each side for 1 minute or until brown flecks appear. Press the edges of the chapati with a clean tea-towel while cooking to help air bubbles form.

5 As chapatis are cooked, wrap in a cloth to keep them hot.

Makes 8

Parathas

2 cups plain flour

1 cup plain wholemeal flour

½ tspn baking powder

2 tspns caster sugar

1 egg, lightly beaten

125 g (4 oz) ghee, melted

cold water to mix

extra ghee for frying

1 Sift flours and baking powder into a mixing bowl, add sugar, beaten egg and 2 tablespoonsful of the melted ghee and mix well. Add enough cold water to mix to a firm dough. Turn dough out onto a lightly floured board, knead lightly and shape mixture into a ball. Wrap dough in plastic wrap and stand for 2 hours.

2 Pinch off large pieces of dough and roll out to thin rounds, about 11 cm (4 in) in diameter. Brush liberally with remaining melted ghee.

3 Make a cut from the centre of the round out to the edge, and roll up tightly to form a cone. Pick up the cone in your hand and press the point and the base together, and flatten slightly. You will now have a flattened circle of dough with a spiral pattern.

Chapatis with Curried Scones

4 Roll out again on a lightly floured board to about 4 mm (⅛ in) thickness, being careful not to press the air out of the sides of the rounds.

5 Melt a little extra ghee in a heavy-based frying pan, add parathas and cook until golden brown on both sides, about 4 minutes. Drain on absorbent paper before serving.

Makes about 22

Sesame Curried Biscuits

2 tblspns sesame seeds

185 g (6 oz) butter or margarine

1½ cups finely grated tasty cheddar cheese

¼ cup grated parmesan cheese

1½ cups plain flour

1 tspn salt

1 tspn curry powder

1 Toast sesame seeds in dry frying pan until golden brown. Spread on plate to cool.

2 Beat butter and grated cheeses together until combined, add sesame seeds and mix well. Sift flour, salt and curry powder and mix thoroughly into butter mixture.

3 Divide dough in half. Shape each piece into a roll about 4 cm (2 in) in diameter. Wrap in foil or plastic wrap and place in freezer until ready to use.

4 Slice thinly and place on baking trays, bake in a moderate oven (180°C) for 12 minutes or until golden and cooked. Leave to cool on baking trays.

Makes 50–60

Pappadams

These spicy wafers come in packets of 25 and 50. Fry one at a time in 2 cm (1 in) of oil until they puff up and turn golden – just a few seconds in hot oil. Then drain on absorbent paper. Store in an airtight container or plastic bag.

SWEET TASTE SENSATION

After a hot and spicy dish, what better way to end a meal than a light and refreshing dessert.

Kheer Kamala

6 large oranges

6 cups milk

½ cup sugar

⅓ cup finely chopped almonds

few drops rosewater

1 Using a vegetable peeler thinly peel one orange and cut the peel into thin shreds (for decoration). Place orange shreds in a bowl and cover with boiling water. Set aside for 20 minutes. Peel the remaining oranges and discard the peel.

2 Remove all the membrane and pith from the oranges then separate oranges into segments. Arrange segments in a serving dish, set aside while preparing the sauce.

3 Place milk, sugar and almonds in a large, heavy-based saucepan and cook simmering over low heat until milk has reduced to half its original volume and has thickened slightly, about 30 minutes. Stir the mixture occasionally to prevent milk from sticking to the base of the pan.

4 Cook milk to room temperature, stir in rosewater and pour over orange segments. Refrigerate. To serve, garnish with the drained orange shreds and fresh or canned mandarin segments if liked.

Serves 6–8

Milk Puffs in Rose Syrup

1⅓ cups full-cream milk powder

½ cup self-raising flour

½ tspn ground cardamom

2 tspns caster sugar

45g (1½ oz) ghee, melted

cold water to mix

FILLING

1 tblspn sugar

few drops red food colouring

ghee or oil for frying

SYRUP

1 cup sugar

2 cups water

rosewater to taste

1 Sift milk powder, flour and cardamom into a bowl. Add sugar and mix well. Stir in melted ghee, mix until well combined. Gradually add enough cold water to mix to a soft dough.

2 Mix sugar and red food colouring together until well combined.

Top picture: Milk Puffs in Rose Syrup (front), Fudgy Cashew Squares and Kheer Kamala. Right: Melon and Strawberry Sorbet (page 72).